ENGLISH FARMERS
AND THE
POLITICS OF
PROTECTION
1815-1852

MIRROR IMAGE EDITIONS

Harvester Press announces this new series of scholarly books, reproduced direct from camera-ready typescript. Mirror Image Editions will maintain the highest academic standards, and titles will be selected for their original contribution and their intellectual importance.

Mirror Image Editions is we believe, a sensible and necessary response to the unfortunate fact that inflationary pressures and the severe cuts in library budgets make it difficult to publish certain specialised scholarly work. Yet it must be published if at all possible. The concept of Mirror Image Editions will make such manuscripts viable in publishing terms and enable scholars to reach their audience in book form.

We shall be pleased to consider proposals for Mirror Image Editions, in any subject in which we currently publish. We will accept manuscripts in camera-ready form, and will advise authors on the preparation of typescripts.

Mirror Image Editions are reproduced by lithography, and bound in hard covers with a fully finished jacket. Edition sizes are normally expected to range from 500 to 1,000 copies. Each title will be separately published in the United States. We will only include a title in the Mirror Image series after it has been subject to exactly the same editorial reading which we apply to all our other books.

ENGLISH FARMERS AND THE POLITICS OF PROTECTION

1815-1852

TRAVIS L. CROSBY

Professor of History, Wheaton College, Massachusetts

THE HARVESTER PRESS

First published in 1977 by
THE HARVESTER PRESS LIMITED
Publisher: John Spiers
2 Stanford Terrace,
Hassocks, Sussex, England

Copyright © Travis L. Crosby 1977

ISBN 0 85527 116 7

Printed in Great Britain by
REDWOOD BURN LIMITED
Trowbridge & Esher

Table of Contents

Acknowledgements

Research on this topic began as a doctoral dissertation under David Spring at the Johns Hopkins University. I benefitted greatly from Professor Spring's initial guidance. I also owe much to F.M.L. Thomson for his encouragement and his many kindnesses. Without Richard W. Davis, Norman Gash, Earnest John Knapton, Richard Olney, and Jane Ruby, this book would have been less readable than it is. John Spiers of Harvester Press took extraordinary care in providing thoughtful criticisms of the manuscript.

One of the most pleasant tasks in the preparation of this book was the time spent in the archives and libraries of England and the United States. Unfailingly helpful, their staffs facilitated in every way possible my research. My thanks go to the British Museum, the Public Record Office, the University of London Library, the Institute of Historical Research, the National Trust at Hughenden, the Library of Congress, and the Libraries of Harvard University and the Johns Hopkins University. Of the local record offices visited in England, I wish to acknowledge in particular the Berkshire Record Office, the Cornwall Record Office, the Essex Record Office, and the Lincolnshire Record Office.

I should like to express a special note of thanks to the National Endowment for the Humanities and to Wheaton College for making it possible to spend several months at the University of Reading. The congenial atmosphere provided by the University and the Institute of Agricultural History at Reading enabled me to make substantial progress at a crucial time in the preparation of this book. E.L. Jones and E.J.T. Collins were especially helpful at Reading.

My thanks to Nancy Shepardson, Joan Silva, Cathy Rogers, and Alice Peterson of Wheaton College for typing the manuscript.

Finally, I am greatly indebted to my wife, Faye, who labored long over the preparation of the appendices, who clarified ambiguities, and who helped in the other ways that authors will understand. To her the book is dedicated.

Chapter I Farmers and Politics

The impact of the Industrial Revolution upon English society is well
known. Less well remembered has been its impact upon historical studies.
The rapid growth of a factory system and large urban communities with all
its attendant problems has directed historians' attention so much toward
the city that the countryside has been neglected. In particular the study of
English rural politics has suffered. Contrasted to the noisy and often
violent urban electorate, rural voters seemed tame, even uninteresting.
This has been put down to a dominant landowning class which exerted its
power above all to preserve social and political order. Great landlords
and country gentry thus were thought to dictate the terms of politics: the
lesser landlords, gentry, and farmers obeyed. The unenfranchised mass of
agricultural laborers scarcely counted.

Research in recent years, however, has shown that beneath the apparent
calm of village life in the nineteenth century were currents of discontent
that occasionally erupted into violence. Much of the research has emphasized
the role of the agricultural laborer.[1] This has complemented the work of
historians who have examined the role of the aristocracy and gentry at the
upper end of the rural social scale.[2] But there has been a curious omission
in recent work on rural English politics: there has been little examination
of the role of the farmer. It is a curious omission since farmers were the
largest group of rural voters throughout most of the nineteenth century.
They were also the closest approximation to a middle class in rural England.
They were men of thrusting ambition, of political and social aims no less
than the grandees or the laborers. Why, then, have farmers been ignored?

The reason for omission lies in the fact that farmers have been considered as political appendages of their landlords. Nowhere has the idea
of the deferential voter seemed more applicable than to farmers.[3] Dependent

upon the good will of their landlords for the continutation of their tenancies, farmers have seemed to be at the beck and call of their economic superiors. In short, it was thought that to study the political opinions of farmers one needed only to examine the opinions of landholders. There is, of course, some truth in this. Any reader of estate papers can produce evidence that some landlords did exert a strict political control over their tenantry. It would be incorrect, however, to assume this was always the case. There were special circumstances which from time to time overturned established patterns of rural politics. In times of economic or social unrest political opinion and influence might well work from the rural constituencies upward. On these occasions farmers, not unlike members of the urban electorate, organized themselves into political pressure groups.[4] The aim of this study is to show how these pressure groups originated in the early nineteenth century and how they contributed to the development of farmers as an active political force. It will become obvious that farmers' agitations belie the notion of a deferential rural electorate. But it will also be clear that farmers did not seek to displace traditional country leadership. Rather, farmers wanted merely to spur on those whom they considered their natural leaders. Farmers wanted the aristocracy and the gentry to carry out more energetically their traditional role--the protection of the land.

Farmers were able to exert influence because of their economic power. By the early nineteenth century farmers had won a recognized economic position in the countryside. Since the sixteenth century, farming had slowly improved as more sophisticated practices were diffused throughout the country; better fertilizer, increased crop rotation, irrigation, and the enclosure of land all played important roles.[5] Central to these practices was an entrepreneurial

partnership of mutual advantage between landlord and farmer, the former
providing necessary capital and the latter implementing the actual improvements. In the last half of the eighteenth century agricultural improvement
was accelerated by a purely fortuitous but decisive upturn in prices culminating in the high prices during the Napoleonic Wars.[6] Farmers experienced
an unprecedented boom.

By mid-century, it is fair to say that farmers occupied an economic
position in English rural society no less important than that of the
aristocracy. As producers, they fed the mushrooming populations of the new
industrial towns. As consumers, they contributed significantly to the demand
that helped promote industrial growth. Indeed, it has been suggested that
a higher proportion of farmers' incomes were available for expenditure on
manufactured goods than was the case with the non-agricultural middle class
since farmers had lower food and housing expenditures.[7] The importance of
the economic role of farmers has never been better stated than in an anonymous
leader of The Times, written in 1850. Claiming that farmers held the
"principal pass" of England's economic system, The Times wrote that:

> In half an hour's walk from every market place in
> the kingdom you find yourself under the sway of these
> powerful and responsible, though unassuming potentates.
> Once among green fields and hedgerows, and the tenant-
> farmer is your immediate superior. The road you are
> riding upon, the ditch you leap over, and the bridge you
> cross, are maintained by him. If you damage a fence,
> it is his. The cattle are his. The labourers are in his
> pay, and the cottages are in his letting. He keeps the
> carpenter's bench, the sawpit, and the forge incessantly

at work. The village shop and the village public-
house are filled by his servants and his labourers.
If profits fall, he has to draw on his capital to keep
things going. If wages are reduced, he has to bear
the odium. If disaffection spreads, his ricks are
burnt. When he can no longer pay wages, he must
still pay rates.[8]

As the quote above indicates the term "farmer" usually meant tenant
farmer--that is one who did not own his own land, but rented from a landlord. Some farmers, of course, did own their land while others owned some
and rented some. Since the late eighteenth century, however, most agricultural land was held and farmed by tenants.[9] The period of high prices
had accelerated a movement from smaller owner-occupied farms to larger
rental units. Small landowners--the fabled yeoman of English history--by
selling out and using the capital to stock a large rental farm could increase
the amount of crops grown and hence profits. Between farmers of all types
(whether owner or renter or both), however, there was a common economic
interest in agricultural improvement and in maintaining high prices for
agricultural produce.

A clear distinction could be made between large and small farmers.
William Marshall, perhaps the most acute of rural observers, noted in 1790
the contribution of large farmers to rural society. "Every district," he
wrote, "has its leading men; its 'capital farmers': their proportionate
number varying, in some degree at least, with the size of farms prevalent
within it, and the state of husbandry at which it has arrived." These
capital farmers, continued Marshall:

...have many advantages over the lower orders of
husbandmen. They travel much; especially those
whose principal object is livestock. They are led
to distant markets, and perhaps to the metropolis.
They see, of course, various modes of management,
and mix in various companies; consisting not merely
of men of their own profession: men of fortune
and science have, in late years, admitted them into
their company: and to their mutual advantage. Thus
their prejudices are worn off, their knowledge enlarged, and their dispositions rendered liberal and
communicative, in a degree which these, who have not
mixed and conversed freely with them, are not aware of.[10]

The size of farm was not the only criterion of a large farmer. The
type of crop grown and proximity to markets were equally important. For example, a small farm near London growing specialized crops such as fruit or
hops might well have a higher value than a large cattle or sheep farm in
remoter districts. Farm sizes alone, then, can be a misleading statistic:
nevertheless, it is the most convenient method of categorization. To obtain
an approximate number of farms and their size at mid-century, the census of
1851 may be used.[11] Small farms of less than 100 acres numbered 116, 163
in 1851.[12] Middle-sized farms of 100 to 300 acres numbered 55,073. The
largest farms, of 300 or more acres, numbered 13, 184. In short, a fair number, about thirty-seven percent of the whole, of middling to large farms
existed in England in 1851. Within that number were many who would fit
Marshall's definition of capital farmers.

In addition to their economic striving, farmers sought to win a social
status commensurate with their affluence. Better education for their sons,
more finery for their daughters, and larger kitchens for their wives were
obvious ambitions.[13] Symbolic of farmers' rising status was their penetra-
tion of that formerly aristocratic pastime, the fox-hunt. "Smartly turned
out tenant farmers" often hunted with the Brocklesby in Lincolnshire.[14] In
Essex some farmers owned packs of hounds, the most notable among them the
Essex Invincibles.[15] Such social striving by farmers drew an amused comment
from the country gentleman and novelist R. S. Surtees. One of his characters in Ask Mama was the arriviste farmer, John Hybrid of Barley Hill Farm,
who, as he paid his respects to the hunt leader of the first day of the
hunting season, revealed his rough origins by "bowing and stepping and
bowing and stepping as if he was measuring off a drain." But it should be
noted that Farmer Hybrid captures the attractive (and fortune hunting)
Miss de Glancey by the novel's end.

Some idea of the energy and enterprise that characterize farmers of
this age may be obtained from a few examples. A notable Suffolk farming
family were the Biddles. Arthur Biddle (1783-1860) of Playford, near Ipswich,
took a farm of 250 acres from the Marquis of Bristol while still a young man.[16]
Remaining at Hill Farm until his death, he gradually increased his holding
until he rented a total of a thousand acres at one time. Biddell was also
a land surveyor and the inventor of such formidable sounding agricultural
implements as Biddell's Scarifier and Biddell's Extirpating Harrow. All four
of Biddell's sons had successful careers as farmers or engineers; William,
the third son, became M.P. for West Suffolk in the 1870's and was known as
the "Tenant Farmer's M.P."[17]

The Tabor family of Essex was another of those prosperous, upwardly mobile farming families that characterized this age.[18] John Tabor (1728-1815) farmed Harmas and Aylwards under Lord Nugent, and had a reputation as a shrewd man of business. Once, when wheat prices were rising rapidly, Tabor sought and obtained permission from a reluctant Lord Nugent to plow up parkland and lay it down to wheat. Early the following morning before Nugent was awake and could change his mind Tabor had collected men and plows and cultivated numerous acres. His son, John English Tabor (1771-1846), continued acquiring land until he farmed 560 acres of his own and leased some to other tenants.

Another important Essex farming family were the Parkers. Christopher Comyns Parker (1774-1843) had begun his farming career at the age of twenty-two, taking Woodham Mortimer Place in 1796.[19] By 1826 he held 450 acres in Woodham Mortimer and surrounding parishes, most of which was rental. Eventually Parker farmed some two thousand acres and had the management--in his role as estate agent--of another twenty thousand acres. Parker was active in local political affairs, serving as Chairman of the Maldon Board of Guardians and once as mayor of Maldon. His son, John Oxley Parker (1812-1887), increased the leaseholds of his father as well as purchasing more land in several parishes, part of which estate still remains in the hands of the Parker family.

One of the largest farmers in England at mid-century was Richard Dawson of Withcall, Lincolnshire.[20] Leased from Lord Willoughby, his farm extended for more than 2500 acres, virtually the whole of the parish. It was well cultivated arable land and had made Dawson a wealthy man; the value of the land was set in 1842 at Ƚ84,959. Apart from the agricultural value of the land, the farm was well stocked with game and had a reputation of being the best coursing ground in England. Another large farmer, Samuel Jonas of Icleton, Cambridgeshire, held over 2000 acres.[21] An active improver, he was a member of the Council of the Royal Agricultural Society from its foundation in 1839, and won its prize for the best report on the farming of Cambridgeshire. He was also active in advocating farmers' political and economic programs in the 1840's.

Wealthy and respectable farmers of the sort we have described were conscious of their responsible position in the countryside and proud of their achievements. There were men difficult to intimidate. Sensible landlords did not attempt to do so. It was more fruitful in the long run for the landlord to maintain a happy working relationship with his tenants. Too great a political demand upon one's tenantry could detract from the chief purpose of an agricultural estate which was after all economic. As the ideal of agricultural improvement had spread since the eighteenth century, and landed estates were regarded more and more by their proprietors with a business eye, efficient farming was at a premium. Landlords would be reluctant to remove an active, improving farmer whatever his political convictions. In any case, tradition in many parts of the country (as in Lincolnshire) worked against the removal of tenants unless there were exceptional circumstances.[22]

That many farmers felt secure in their tenancies is evident from the demands--such as rent reduction or the undertaking of improvements--which they occasionally made upon their landlords. Ironically enough, agricultural depression often enhanced farmers' bargaining position vis-à-vis their landlords. In a time of falling profits for farmers, landlords could ultimately be affected. If landlords did not reduce rents or otherwise accommodate their tenants, the tenants might stop rental payments, or surrender their leases.

Thus, given the weakened economic position of their landlords, farmers could exert an influence of surprising proportions. A realization among farmers of their latent economic strength, especially during the post-1815 depressions, contributed directly to their political self-confidence and independence. The papers of the sixth Lord Monson during the depression of 1850-52 fully exemplify the awkward position of a landlord in the face of a recalcitrant tenantry. Some of Monson's tenants adopted an almost abusive tone in their demands for rent reduction, or for landlord-financed improvements. Monson's supervistory agent, Harvey Gem, sympathized with Monson at his "awakening to such ugly sights as tenants and agents letters in such days as these...."[23] But Gem also cautioned Monson that he would be unable to withstand too great a loss of his tenantry, "for a deep purse would be needed to meet a general strike."[24]

Generally speaking, then, threats to farmers' economic security did not come from strained landlord-tenant relations over political matters. Farmers themselves believed that the greatest threat to their livelihood came from a came from a series of agricultural depressions after 1815. The worst times were the early 1820's, the mid-1830's and the early 1850's. Although the depressions worked unevenly throughout the country, affecting the clay regions more than the light-soiled regions, they were severe enough to frighten most farmers.[25] Farmers who had begun extensive improvement during the war years, or who had undertaken long leases at high rents, now faced the prospect of a declining agricultural market. They believed that continued agricultural improvement and efficient farming could not offset their losses.

Grumbling at farmers' ordinaries on market day was no solution to the problem. The conviction grew among farmers that only through organization and agitation directed toward parliament could their grievances be redressed.

Farmers sought to bring pressure to bear on parliament in a number
of ways. County meetings offered one means of catching the attention of
parliament. County meetings were recognized by no statute and seem to have
evolved through customary usage.[26] Meetings were requested by signed
requisitions which were then presented to the sheriff, who in turn convened the meeting and presided over it.[27] County meetings could also be
summoned on the authority of any seven magistrates of the county. Tradi-
tionally, county meetings could be called for a variety of reasons. Nomin-
ations for knights of the shire at election times took place at county meetings.
In war, they often were called to discuss means of providing for local
defence. Any matter of local importance could, in fact, initiate a county
meeting. They were usually held at recognized places in the county, and
until the early nineteenth century only freeholders could speak and vote on
petitions which were then sent to parliament. Thus, county meetings formed
a link between the countryside and parliament.

A substantial change of emphasis in county meetings occurred in the late
eighteenth century: they were convened more frequently for specifically
political purposes. The Yorkshire Association, an important pressure group
of the 1780's, used them extensively to promote its program of reform. Indeed, for Christopher Wyvill and the leaders of the Association, county meetings were "the ultimate spring of authority for their activities."[28] After
1815, the use of county meetings as forums for political debate seems to
have accelerated. Not only were county meetings becoming more political;
their composition was changing as well. The idea that only a restricted
part of the population--the nobility, gentry, clergy, and freeholders--could
participate in county meetings was attacked with increasing success in the
early years of the nineteenth century. It appears that Cornwall pioneered

the removal of attendance restrictions at county meetings. Under the leadership of a reforming Whig, Sir John Colman Rashleigh, a movement to open
county meetings to all inhabitants began in 1814.[29] The attack by Rashleigh
and other reformers on restricted county meetings clearly benefitted the
landless tenant farmers. Easing of attendance restrictions at county meetings
meant that the control formerly exerted at these meetings by the landed
classes became less effective. Now that meetings were opening to all inhabitants of the counties, landlords could no longer rely on a deferential
rural gathering. That English farmers generally were eager to participate,
even to initiate, county meetings will be evident in this study.

More important as a means of disseminating farmers' opinions at a local
and national level were the agricultural improvement societies. Agricultural
societies had at first grown only slowly. In 1800 there were sixty
societies since the first had been established in 1723: by the 1840's
there were several times that number.[30] Among the most important
national and regional societies were the Bath and West of England Society
established in 1778, the Board of Agriculture established in 1793, and the
Smithfield Club established in 1798.[31] There were also smaller, more local
societies organized at the county, hundred, district, or even village level.
County societies often prompted subsidiary organizations. The Essex Agricultural Society, for example, had eight regional districts, each with its
own headquarters. Those giving a half guinea annual subscription became
members of the district society; another half guinea entitled them to membership in the county society.[32] Members' subscriptions constituted the oper-
ating funds of the societies. Without such subscriptions the societies could
not have continued their main activity--the offering of cash prizes or pieces
of plate to deserving farmers and laborers. Not unmindful of the literary

talents of their members, some societies also sponsored essay contests on
agricultural subjects. The early societies often combined welfare and benefit programs for the poor along with projects designed to spur agricultural
improvement. Nevertheless, the sponsoring of stock shows, wool fairs, and
the encouragement of better agricultural practices remained the main intent
of these societies until well into the nineteenth century.

It is unclear how much these societies contributed to the cult of agricultural improvement among farmers in the first half of the nineteenth
century. Very probably they helped diffuse information on the latest techniques among farmers as a whole. More important for our purpose is their
role during times of agricultural depression, for then the talk at the
meetings turned from scientific farming to political agitation. Thus, the
improvement societies provided convenient forums for aggrieved farmers. In
many instances, the societies were reconstituted as political pressure groups.

Both county meetings and agricultural societies were an effective means
of bringing together the members of an inherently solitary occupation such
as farmers. But these meetings were at best periodic affairs, the proceedings
of which might not reach every concerned farmer. To inform
a wider rural audience, some vehicle capable of maintaining a
sustained flow of information was needed. Country newspapers filled this
need admirably. They did so in three ways: by carrying the proceedings of
the agricultural societies and county meetings; by transmitting local
opinion in letters to the editors; and by advocating agricultural policies
in their editorial columns. Provincial in character and catering to a county
readership, these newspapers were less sophisticated than their metropolitan
counterparts. This fact caused the London papers, such as _The Times_, to underestimate the appeal and potential influence of the county papers. But the

provincial newspaper had undergone a dramatic change in the early years of
the nineteenth century. No longer composed by a scissors and paste method
or published by men who were chiefly printers, the provincial newspaper had
become by 1830 an important vehicle of rural opinion.[33]

It is obvious that meetings and newspapers provided the tools for a successful campaign among farmers. Before farmers could become an effective pressure
group, however, it was necessary for them to form a bond of unity, and to
have a sense of themselves as a distinct interest group. An overriding issue
was necessary. There were numerous alternatives which could possibly have
provided a central issue around which farmers might rally. These included
farmers' opposition to various taxes, to tithes, and to the poor rate. But
none of these, as we shall see, proved an effective focus of farmers' discontent. Farmers' economic interests were not always in harmony. Opposition to
the malt tax, for example, was a matter of primary concern for barley farmers.
First imposed in 1697, the malt tax had risen from slightly more than 6d. a
bushel to 4s. 5d. a bushel by 1815. The increasing importance of the tax as a
source of revenue to the government can be seen in these comparative net
yields: in 1793 the yield was £1,203,000 and in 1815 it was £6,044,276.[34]
Barley growers were affected because the brewing industry, which normally
was the largest consumer of barley, had reduced its demand in the face of
the rising malt tax: brewers began to use less expensive substitutes to give
beer the desired malty flavor. The high malt tax also discouraged the farmer
as a home brewer, previously an established practice in the countryside. Barley growers believed that a repeal of the malt tax would benefit them substan-
tially, and they therefore supported various anti-malt tax movements throughout
the nineteenth century. Another tax affecting a different set of farmers was
the salt tax, which gave offence to stock and dairy farmers who used salt as
an animal condiment. Dairy farmers also used salt as a preservative in their butter and cheese. By 1805, the tax had been raised to 15s. the bushel, making

it a very heavy impost-thirty times the actual price of salt.[35] Not surprisingly, Cheshire, Shropshire, and other dairy counties took the lead in
trying to bring about its abolition in the early years of the nineteenth
century.[36] A third tax, affecting even a smaller number of farmers, was
the hop tax. Hop growing was concentrated in two counties, Kent and
Sussex, with smaller acreages in Hereford. This concentration of a majority of England's hop growers was an aid to organization, and Kent was the
center of hop farmers' agitation after the Napoleonic Wars. It seems
the Kentish growers had a rudimentary organization though little evidence
of it remains. Petitioning parliament was a frequent activity.[37]

None of these government taxes could provide a sustained focus of
discontent. They were too localized and did not affect every farmer equally.
A more widespread grievance among farmers and one that brought better
prospects for unity was the poor rate. From an average of £2 million
annually in the decades before the Napoleonic Wars, the poor rate had
risen steadily to £ 7,870,801 in 1818. And since the rate was assessed
not upon the owners of land but upon the occupiers, most of the burden
fell upon tenant farmers. But once again, the poor rate operated unevenly: it varied greatly from country to country. Even among the counties
which had a high poor rate farmers realized that the poor had to be
supported.[38] Another traditional grievance among farmers was the tithe
system. Agricultural opposition to tithes had begun in earnest during the
seventeenth and eighteenth centuries when the movement for agricultural
improvement was beginning. Although there were lay as well as ecclesiastical tithe owners, tithers' antipathy seems to have been directed
mainly to the latter. Perhaps the reason for this was that lay

owners were less dependent on tithes than the clergy and hence less demanding. Farmers were provoked by several aspects of the tithe system. It was levied not on clear profits but on total produce. It was a system which, from the point of view of the commercial farmer, allowed a sleeping partner to share in the gains of husbandry without risking any capital--someone who always claimed a tenth of the results accruing from improved methods and the growth of new crops. The method of collecting tithes was especially irritating. The farmer had to give notice to the tithe owner of his intention to harvest in order that he or his tithe proctor could attend. During the harvest, the tithe owner or proctor marked every tenth hay or corn shock which had to be left where it stood until the entire field was completely ricked. Every tenth pig, lamb, fowl, egg, cabbage, or other fruit or vegetable had to be set apart in the same manner. Any default in giving notice, or interfering with the proctor would render the tithers liable to the Ecclesiastical Courts, which were often dilatory and expensive. Even so, dissension between Anglican clergymen and farmers often went as far as the courts. J. A. Venn, who studied reports of the legal cases concerning tithes from the fourteenth to the nineteenth centuries, was surprised that agriculture could be carried on "under such incessant friction as took place between the clergy and the farmers...."[39]

The question of tithes, however, was too clouded with religious complexities to serve as an effective rallying cry for a national farmers' movement. Whereas nonconformist farmers would naturally be strongly opposed to tithes, Anglicans would ultimately be reluctant to push too hard at something that might strike so close to the heart of the established church. In any case, much of the bad feeling over tithes was declining by the 1830's as the practice grew of substituting cash payment for payment in kind.[40]

An issue which avoided many of the disadvantages of those discussed above was the currency question. In 1797, Pitt had suspended cash payments of the Bank of England as a war time exigency. This allowed the government to issue plentiful supplies of paper money. In 1819, however, Peel's Act allowed the Bank to resume cash payments. This return to gold had generally a favorable result in England's foreign exchange position but its domestic consequences were more controversial. It seems that the deflationary tendency of the act contributed to a depression already underway.[41]

Farmers felt the impact of Peel's Act directly through their local country banks. In prosperous times the banks willingly loaned money to farmers to tide them over the harvest period, to make improvements, or to pay their rent. The end of agricultural prosperity, however, combined with the restriction of note issues after 1819, made the bankers reluctant to continue advances to farmers--especially to tenant farmers, who could not offer sufficient security. This led some farmers to believe that a repeal of Peel's Act would bring a return to the expansionary times they experienced during the war. The issue proved an enduring one, but it was an issue that had limited appeal. The complexities of high fiscal policy were not readily understood by many farmers. It is unlikely that smaller farmers, especially, would be as interested in an issue that was designed to aid the larger, improving farmers.

An issue which found a brief popularity among farmers was, surprisingly enough, parliamentary reform. Exasperated by what they felt to be parliamentary insensitivity to their economic plight, farmers flirted temporarily in the early 1820's with Radical and Whig agitators who promised them that reform of parliament would insure relief for the farmers. This issue never developed further, however, for it represented a fit of pique more than a deeply felt conviction.

Although each of the issues discussed above provided some focus for
farmers' agitations, none proved as popular or as enduring as agricultural
protection. Protection was an issue which, as we shall see, could appeal
to large and small farmer, to nonconformist and Anglican, to stock and arable
farmer, to tenant and owner-occupier alike. The idea of unity among farmers
against foreign producers had enormous appeal to xenophobic English farmers.
Prohibiting foreign agricultural imports seemed a simple and natural solution
to the problem of falling agricultural prices. There was some truth to
farmers' contention that agricultural imports had been increasing. Wheat
imports, for example, rose sharply during the war years--from 854,000 quarters
in 1796 to nearly a million and a half quarters in 1810. Although wheat imports fell back for a time after the war, they rose again to an annual
average of more than 1, 400,000 quarters during the 1830's. However, farmers
failed to realize that consumption outpaced imports. As late as the 1840's,
the proportion of the population fed on foreign wheat was lower than three
decades earlier.[42] Low agricultural prices had more to do with expanded
acreage and the growth of efficient farming than imports of foreign grain.

Protection, of course, had a wider appeal than merely to farmers. For
all those who believed that the constitution in church and state was based
essentially upon the land, agricultural protection was an article of faith.
The established clergy favored protection because it seemed to support agricultural prosperity which was necessary to the tithe system. Gentry and
aristocracy of both parties favored protection as necessary to maintain the
preponderance of the landed classes. Most important, protection had long
been the official policy of governments. Since medieval times agricultural
protection had been enshrined in the Corn Laws.[43] Originally, Corn Laws
were designed to regulate stocks of grain in the country to insure adequate

supplies and fair prices to both consumer and grower. By the early nineteenth century, the Corn Laws had become more favorable to the grower. This
reflected governmental concern that England produce sufficient food in wartime. Both the 1791 and 1804 Corn Laws, by allowing importation only at high
duties, encouraged the growth of domestic corn. The 1815 Corn Law was even
more protectionist in intent, for it prohibited all importation when domestic
prices were below certain levels (although beyond these high price levels,
corn was allowed free entry).

Of all the groups interested in protection farmers remained the most
fervent. For them the necessity of protection was not based upon vague
generalities purporting to be for the national good: it was essential to
their livelihood. Their remedy for falling prices after 1815 was more
protection. They established protectionist societies throughout the country
in the 1820's to induce parliament to strengthen the Corn Laws. When depression returned in the 1830's, they adopted similar tactics. The establishment of the Anti-Corn Law League in 1838, with its program of free trade,
intensified the protectionist controversy. To arable farmers, especially,
the prospect of a free trade in corn was unthinkable. In response to the
League, protectionist societies expanded in the 1840's. They were especially
active in bringing protectionist pressure to bear upon their parliamentary
representatives. As we know, the protectionists failed to prevent Corn Law
repeal in 1846. But a majority of the Conservative party, stiffened by a
protectionist constituency, rebelled against its leadership in 1846, and
brought to a brief period of influence a Protectionist party. The backbone
of the party and its chief basis of support were farmers. By providing a
political outlet at a national level, the Protectionist party further schooled

the farmers in the politics of public opinion. It thus helped bring to
the deliberations of Westminster the opinions of an important rural class
and in so doing contributed to the development of the political nation.

Footnotes to Introduction

1. See, for example, A. J. Peacock, Bread or Blood (London, 1965); Eric Hobsbawm and George Rude, Captain Swing (London, 1969); J.P.D. Dunbabin, Rural Discontent in Nineteenth-Century Britain (London, 1974).

2. Of which the most important have been the various works of Professor David Spring and Professor F.M.L. Thompson.

3. D. C. Moore has been the most consistent exponent of a deferential rural electorate: see, for example, his "Social Structure, Political Structure and Public Opinion in Mid-Victorian England," in Robert Robson (ed.), Ideas and Institutions of Victorian Britain (New York, 1967), pp. 20-57.

4. Two important recent works which incidentally touch upon farmers' organizations are Richard W. Davis, Political Change and Continuity, 1760-1885: A Buckinghamshire Study (Newton Abbot, 1972); and R. J. Olney, Lincolnshire Politics, 1832-1885 (Oxford U., 1973).

5. Historians tend to view this agricultural change in revolutionary terms; its timing, however, is a matter of debate. Eric Kerridge's, The Agricultural Revolution (London, 1967) argues that it occurred during the sixteenth and seventeenth centuries. J. D. Chambers and G. E. Mingay, The Agricultural Revolution, 1750-1880 (London, 1966) plump for the eighteenth and nineteenth centuries, while Professor Thompson, more cautiously, sees three agricultural revoltuions (F. M. L. Thompson, "The Second Agricultural Revolution, 1815-1880," Econ. Hist. Rev., 2d ser., vol. XXI, no. 1 (April, 1968), pp. 62-77.

6. A. H. John, "Farming in Wartime: 1793-1815," in E. L. Jones and G. E. Mingay (eds.), Land, Labour, and Population in the Industrial Revolution (London, 1967), pp. 28-47.

7.   F. M. L. Thompson, "Landownership and Economic Growth in England
in the Eighteenth Century," in E. L. Jones and S. J. Woolf (eds.), Agrarian
Change and Economic Development (London, 1960), p. 60.

8.   The Times, Dec. 23, 1850. I am indebted to Dr. E. L. Jones for
calling my attention to this passage.

9.   See E. Davies, "The Small Landowners, 1780-1832, in the Light of
the Land Tax Assessments," Econ. Hist. Rev., 1st ser., vol. I (1927), where
he notes that by 1780 the occupying owners (including freeholders, copyholders, and leasees for lives) "had ceased to be an outstanding feature of
English rural economy" (P. 110). Davies estimates that by 1780-86, ninety
percent of English farming was carried on by tenants. Thompson concurs:
"In agricultural terms England was overwhelmingly a land of tenant-farmers
by the late eighteenth century..." (F. M. L. Thompson, "The Social Distribution of Landed Property in England since the Sixteenth Century," Econ. Hist.
Rev., 2d ser., vol. XIX, no. 3 (1966), p. 516).

10.   William Marshall, The Rural Economy of the Midland Counties (London,
1790), Vol I, pp. 115-16.

11.   Census of Great Britain, 1851. Parliamentary Papers, LXXXVIII
(1852-3), pp. 120-802, passim.

12.   Farm size designations are suggested by G. E. Mingay, Enclosure and
the Small Farmer in the Age of the Industrial Revolution (London, 1968), p. 15.

13.   See G. E. Mingay, English Landed Society in the Eighteenth Century
(London, 1963), ch. X, "The Life of the Farmers."

14. F. M. L. Thompson, English Landed Society in the Nineteenth Century (London, 1963), pp. 149-50. It has been suggested that farmers' grievances against the game laws lay less in the capricious destruction of their crops by landlord-led hunts than in a desire for the sporting privileges themselves. See Norman H. Pollock, "The English Game Laws in the Nineteenth Century," (Johns Hopkins University Ph.D. Dissertation, 1968)

15. E. M. Bovill, England in the Age of Nimrod and Surtees (Oxford UP, 1959), p. 39.

16. For information on Biddell, see George Ewart Evans, The Horse in the Furrow (London, 1960), chs. VII-IX.

17. Ibid., p. 163.

18. For the Tabors, see H. S. Tabor, "History of the Tabor Family," (1917); typescript in photocopy form at the Essex Record Office, ERO D/DTa Z6.

19. For the Parkers, see J. Oxley Parker, The Oxley Parker Papers (Colchester, 1964).

20. Details of Dawson's farm are in a description and valuation in the Lincolnshire Record Office, 3 Anc 7/23/43/8, dated 30 April 1842.

21. Select Committee on Agricultural Customs, Parliamentary Papers (1847-48), Vol. VII, pp. 85 ff.

22. See J. A. Perkins, "Tenure, Tenant Right, and Agricultural Progress in Lindsey, 1780-1850," Agric. Hist. Rev., Vol. XXIII, pt. 1 (1975), 1-22.

23. Lincolnshire Record Office, Monson MSS, 25/13/10/3/1, Gem to Monson, Jan. 2, 1851.

24. Ibid., 24/13/10/3/55, Gem to Monson, Apr. 19, 1851.

25. G. E. Fussell and M. Compton, "Agricultural Adjustments after the Napoleonic Wars," Economic History, vol. III, no. 14 (Feb., 1939), p. 188. The claylands were to remain a laggard sector in the agricultural economy

long after 1815: see E. J. T. Collins and E. L. Jones, "Sectoral Advance
in English Agriculture, 1850-1880," <u>Agric. Hist. Rev.</u>, vol. XV, pt. II
(1967), p. 67.

26. The following account of county meetings is taken from B. Keith-
Lucas, "County Meetings," <u>Law Quarterly Rev.</u>, Vol. LXX (Jan., 1954), pp. 109-14.

27. By the nineteenth century, the ancient office of sheriff was more
onerous than honorific. Apart from exposure to public dislike at difficult
county meetings, there were the usual official trivialities that had to be
dealt with, and a not inconsiderable expense. For a high sheriff's activities,
see Cornwall R. O., Rashleigh MSS, DDR (S) 1020-29, pertinent to the term
of office of William Rashleigh in 1820. Also see the accounts of expenses of
Sir Richard Vvyan, Bt., when he was high sheriff in 1840, Cornwall R. O.,
Vyvyan MSS, 22. M/BO/35/31.

28. Ian R. Christie, "The Yorkshire Association, 1780-4: A Study in
Political Organization," <u>The Historical Jnl.</u>, Vol. III (1960), no. 2, p. 149.

29. For Rashleigh and his role in the opening of county meetings, see
"Memoirs of Sir John Colman Rashleigh, Bt., in Four Parts (1772-1847)" in
typescript at the Cornwall Record Office, Truro; and W. Brian Elvins, "The
Reform Movement and County Politics in Cornwall, 1809-1852," (M.A. Thesis,
University of Birmingham, 1959). He was related to the influential Rashleighs
of Menabilly.

30. G. E. Fussell, <u>More Old English Farming Books</u> (London, 1950), p. 20.
Claudio Veliz, "Arthur Young and the English Landed Interest, 1784-1813"
(London School of Economics Ph.D. Thesis, 1959), p. 22.

31. For an account of the Board of Agriculture, see Rosalind Mitchison, "The Old Board of Agriculture (1793-1822)," English Hist. Rev., vol. LXXIV (1959), pp. 41-69. Rosalind Mitchison's Agricultural Sir John (London, 1962) is a biography of the founder of the Board, Sir John Sinclair. A history of the Smithfield Club is Sir B. T. Brandreth Gibbs, The Smithfield Club (London, 1881), 3d ed. For a history of the Bath and West of England Society, see William Lewis, A Century of Agricultural Progress (Bath, 1879).

32. An Account of the Proceedings, Intentions, Resolutions, and Premiums of the Essex Society for the Encouragement of Agriculture and Industry (Bocking, n.d.).

33. See "The Provincial Press," Westminster Review, vol. XII, no. 23 (1830), pp. 69-103.

34. See Stephen Dowell, A History of Taxation and Taxes in England (London, 1888), 2nd (rev.) ed., Vol IV, pp. 72 ff.

35. Ibid., pp. 3 ff.

36. Edward Hughes, Studies in Administration and Finance, 1558-1825 (Manchester, 1934), pp. 468 ff.; Bristol Jnl., Feb. 28, 1818; Salopian Jnl., May 8 and May 29, 1822.

37. Information on hop farming may be found in E. J. Lance, The Hop Farmer (London, 1838); Hubert H. Parker, The Hop Industry (London, 1934); and Peter Mathias, The Brewing Industry in England 1700-1830 (Cambridge, 1959).

38. A concise discussion of the effect of the poor rate upon farmers may be found in Elie Halévy, A History of the English People in the Nineteenth Century (New York, 1949), 2nd (rev.) ed., Vol. I, pp. 377-81, and Vol. II, pp. 40-3.

39. J. A. Venn, _Foundations of Agricultural Economics_ (Cambridge, 1923), p. 100.

40. W. R. Ward, "The Tithe Question in England in the Early Nineteenth Century," _Jnl. of Ecclesiastical History_, Vol. XVI, No. 1 (Apr. 1965), 67-81.

41. A. W. Acworth, _Financial Reconstruction in England, 1815-1822_ (London, 1925), pp. 99ff.; A.H. Imlah, _Economic Elements in the Pax Britannica_ (Harvard, 1958), p. 11; L. S. Pressnell, _Country Banking in the Industrial Revolution_ (Oxford, 1956), p. 247.

42. Chambers and Mingay, _The Agricultural Revolution 1750-1880_ pp. 115, 126.

43. Donald Grove Barnes, _A History of the English Corn Laws from 1660-1846_ (New York, 1930), ch. 1.

Chapter II - The Farmer as Protectionist[1]

The first stirrings of a protectionist movement can be seen as
early as 1814. By December of that year the Farmers' Journal, an
important source of farmers' opinions, devoted several columns of its
issues to letters from distressed farmers. Not only were there the
usual complaints of taxes, poor rates, and tithes, but there was also
an attempt to discover the reason for falling agricultural prices.
Most farmers laid the blame at the door of potential grain imports
from abroad, imports which had hitherto been restricted because of war.
The signing of the Treaty of Ghent on December 24, 1814, ending the
American war meant that grain imports from that part of the world were
again possible.[2] "The account of peace with America so completely
alarmed the dealers in Corn," wrote one Devonshire correspondent to
the Farmers' Journal, "that no business was done at Barnstable last
Friday, nor at Bideford on Tuesday last. . . ."[3] The same opinion was
forthcoming from the East Riding of Yorkshire: "The news of the Peace
with America caused a sad stagnation in the wheat trade in these markets. . . ."[4] Peace with America coupled with peace on the continent
posed a distinct threat, in farmers' minds, to their protected wartime domestic markets. Indeed, wheat had fallen from
an average of 108s. 5d. per quarter in 1813 to 73s. 9d. in 1814, and
stood at 60s. 8d. in January, 1815.

Fearful of this foreign threat to their livelihood, farmers convened to discuss the problem. Letters to newspapers urged farmers at
market towns and in public meetings to sign petitions. Suggested one
such letter: "Numerous petitions, . . .from occupiers and owners of

land, about any market town, will be well received, and well entitled
to the attention of Parliament: they will prevent the inference which
may be drawn from the silence of the farmers, by persons, who will say
that they are not aggrieved, and do not require the interference of
the Legislature, because they make no complaint."[5]

The consensus of the numerous local meetings of agriculturists
throughout the kingdom in the early months of 1815 favored a more protective corn law. A meeting of proprietors and occupiers of land in
the neighborhood of Holbeach, Lincolnshire, declared that the "ruinous
depression" in grain prices was brought about by the importation of
foreign grain.[6] The owners and occupiers of the hundreds of Loddon
and Clavering in Norfolk also blamed the depression of farm prices on
imports.[7] In addition, county meetings were convened denouncing
foreign grain as detrimental to British farmers. A Herefordshire
county meeting assured farmers that their interests were being looked
after. A Colonel Matthews stated that he had information that a new
corn law would soon be enacted whose regulations would "enable the
Farmer to cultivate his land."[8] Meetings were possibly most numerous
in the Fens where farmers, in addition to the usual expenses, had
heavy outlays for drainage. The pages of the Cambridge Chronicle and
the Stamford Mercury are filled with accounts of Fen farmers' meetings.

The intensity of farmers' interest in a more protective corn law
can be further gauged by petitions sent to parliament. There were
143 petitions concerning the corn laws sent to the House of Lords
alone in the first three months of 1815; seventy-one were against any
change in the law and seventy-two prayed for relief, preferably by a

change of the corn law. Of the seventy-two, thirty-five were from "owners and occupiers," twenty-six from "occupiers" or "farmers", four from "owners", and seven were miscellaneous.[9] It would be too much to say that farmers had a major share in the passage of the Corn Law of 1815; the truth of the matter is that a widespread support in the country existed for the bill. But farmers probably strengthened the case for its passage.

However, when it became obvious that the Corn Law for all its protectionism did not halt the downward trend of agricultural prices, many farmers jumped to the conclusion that the law was not restrictive enough: they were amenable to the idea of a newer, even more restrictive corn law. There was also a growing belief that the time had come to establish a permanent farmers' protectionist organization. In January of 1815 an attempt was made to form a national association for the protection of "the Farming Interest." An anonymous handbill was circulated in country regions stating the objectives of the proposed society.[10] Admission would be limited to those whose principal business was farming, who occupied land with an annual valuation of at least one hundred pounds, and who did not "let off" more than one-third of the land they occupied. This attempt at a farmers' organization, the origins of which are shrouded in mystery, never came to fruition, however.

In early 1816 the effects of the agricultural depression brought further consternation to the countryside. Agricultural sentiment was again best mirrored in letters to the Farmers' Journal. If these letters showed much confusion, they also revealed an inchoate awareness that action of some sort was needed. One correspondent who signed himself "A Suffering British Farmer" wrote: "Let us then, one and all, come forward, and earnestly solicit Ministers to take into their serious consideration our present and accumulating distresses. But who will set the machine in motion?--there must be a beginning, we must have a leader."[11]

The task of forming the first farmers' protectionist movement fell to a Bristol solicitor, George Webb Hall. What brief success the movement enjoyed was largely due to his energy and perseverance. The author of innumerable letters and several pamphlets, he was also active in country affairs of every sort. Indeed, as Sir John Sinclair noted in a letter to Arthur Young in 1819, "by his zeal, industry, and talents [he] has become a species of 'Hunt' in agriculture."[12] Unfortunately, little is known about Webb Hall before he entered agrarian politics. It is known, however, that he was born in Bristol in 1765 and lived in or near that city throughout his life. His training in the law prepared him for the sort of varied and influential career which Robson had held up as typical of the rising and respectable profession of the eighteenth-century attorney.[13] At an early age Webb Hall was appointed Chief Clerk to the Court of Requests. Later he became solicitor to the Corporation of Bristol, a post which he retained for twenty-five years. As agent of the Bristol Dock Company, he was instrumental in securing the passage of parliamentary acts for the improvement of the port and harbor; "in fact, [as one obituary put it] Parliamentary business was that to which he had particularly devoted his time, and few were better qualified to surmount those numerous obstacles which are frequently opposed to the progress of such bills."[14]

In addition to pursuing a legal career, Webb Hall was a large-scale farmer who specialized in wool growing. In 1799 he leased Leigh Court, an estate not far from Bristol and two years later he took a second farm near Uxbridge, Somerset. Towards the end of the war he took still another farm, Sneed Park in Gloucestershire, where he spent his last years. He was said to occupy at one time nearly 2300 acres, and to have invested £20,000 in agricultural improvements by 1814.[15] Thus, he was representative of those from outside agriculture who entered farming during the war years with the hope of gaining a share of rising farm profits. Through connections in the Spanish wool trade, Webb Hall began to purchase Merino sheep for his farms; by importing directly from Spain through the port of Bristol he was able to collect a large flock within a short time.[16] On his Uxbridge farm alone it was said that he had 3000 Merinos, thereby making him probably "the largest Merino flockmaster in the kingdom."[17] Lord Sheffield in his annual reports to the Lewes Wool Fair frequently remarked on Webb Hall's zeal for Merino sheep. At the 1812 Fair he commended Webb Hall's "spirited and intelligent exertions" which had brought a gross return of over £2000 for wool sold in September of that year.[18] National recognition for his services to agriculture came in 1820 when he succeeded Arthur Young as Secretary to the Board of Agriculture.

Like other agriculturists, Webb Hall was affected by the post-war agricultural slump. He was especially affected by the growing unpopularity of Merino sheep after 1815; the inability of these indigenously Spanish sheep to adapt to the moist English climate with consequent fatal rot and the poor quality of the mutton seem to have been the main reasons. But Webb Hall was not one to accept passively the economic misfortunes affecting the farming community. Drawing

upon his experiences in farming organizations--he had been a member

of the Board of Agriculture since 1805 and was also a member of the

Bath and West of England Society[19]--he presented a plan of action in

February, 1816. He recommended that a series of county meetings be

held throughout the kingdom with the object of presenting the same

petition to parliament; for "if various Petitions offer contending al-

legations, and conclude each with a different prayer, nothing effectu-

al can be expected."[20] He proposed further that a commitee for each

county be appointed to circulate the petition and to arrange subscrip-

tions for defraying expenses. Finally, he proposed that from the county

committees a general committee of ten or twelve "of the most discreet

and able men" be selected to remain in London to communicate with the

county committee, and to lobby among the members of parliament.[21]

A month after the announcement of this plan, Webb Hall took steps

to implement it. On March 9, 1816, after Lord Somerville's London

cattle show, several owners and occupiers of land who had attended the

show met at the Castle and Falcon Inn and drafted a series of protec-

tionist resolutions to be presented to parliament. The resolutions

asked for a protective duty, equal to thirty percent of the domestic

price, to be levied on certain agricultural imports including wool.[22]

At the close of the meeting, a committee comprising John Martin Cripps

of Surrey, John Ellman of Sussex (son of the noted Southdown sheep

breeder of the same name), and Webb Hall was delegated to remain in

London. The purpose was to impress upon members of parliament the

severity of agricultural distress and to circulate the adopted resolutions throughout England in order to prompt additional protectionist
meetings.[23]

It would seem that during 1816 the committee failed to stir up a
general movement for agricultural protection. Its failure may have
been the result of a lessening of distress--if not for the whole agricultural community, certainly for many of the wheat growers. Wheat
averages moved upwards in 1816 reaching 103s. in December, the result
largely of a poor harvest.[24] Wool prices, however, fell in 1816 and
this may account in part for the continued protectionist agitation among
wool growers led by Webb Hall and his friends. The Merino growers had
a special reason for anxiety in that Merino prices continued to fall
in 1817, unlike the prices of Southdown and Kentish long wool.[25]

It was not unknown for wool growers to complain about the state
regulation of their trade. In the 1780's wool growers in Lincolnshire
had complained about the long standing mercantilist policy which prohibited the export of English wool in order to maintain an ample supply
for the English manufacturer.[26] After 1815, although the rivalry
between wool grower and manufacturer continued, it took a different
form. The wool grower who complained in 1816 was likely to complain
not of his lack of freedom to export so much as of his lack of protection against the foreign wool grower. Imports of raw wool into England
doubled between 1812 and 1814, and the wool grower, like the manufacturer,
demanded the protection of the state.

This protection was refused in April, 1816, when a Select Committee
reported against any alteration in the existing laws.[27] In August at
the Lewes Wool Fair Lord Sheffield deprecated the committee's report

and urged that petitions be sent to parliament asking for a protective
duty on wool. Protectionist resolutions were passed and a committee
appointed, which included the Ellmans, to communicate with other protectionists in the kingdom. A delegation was also selected to attend
a general meeting of wool growers to be held in London in October.[28]

Several weeks before the London meeting Webb Hall again stepped
forward, this time among his neighbors. At a meeting of the landowners
and occupiers of Gloucestershire and Somerset on October 7, he took a
leading part in forming a protective association which adopted resolutions similar to those passed at the Castle and Falcon in March. Webb
Hall and the younger Ellman were among those appointed to a committee
of management.[29] This Gloucester and Somerset Association was probably
the first of the local agricultural protectionist associations which
were soon to become conspicuous in the agitation of the countryside.

Webb Hall and the younger Ellman were again prominent at the wool
growers' meeting in London held on October 29. After resolutions supporting protection for wool had been read, Ellman suggested that the
meeting broaden the resolutions to include all products of the soil.
Webb Hall then carried a motion that the meeting reconstitute itself;
and those who were interested only in wool retired. After an address
by Webb Hall on the need for general agricultural protection, the meeting closed with a decision to ask for an immediate session of parliament
to cope with the agricultural distress.

The movement for general protection, however, again failed to
catch fire. The chief reason was probably the same as before: the
high price of grain. Nevertheless, throughout 1817, Webb Hall continued to propagate his views. By means of the Gloucester and Somerset

Association together with the Farmers' Journal he made known his opinions on the necessity for a duty on all agricultural produce. Indeed, he made a point of deploring the petitions of those wool growers who sought "only a petty selfish protection for wool alone."[30]

Then in late 1817 and early 1818 the rural scene began to change, and Webb Hall found a larger audience. Two things were at work. First, wheat prices began to fall; second, and connected with the fall in prices, corn growers grew anxious about the machinery by which price averages were determined. The younger Ellman voiced this general fear in a series of letters to the Farmers' Journal: he believed that the machinery was at fault, that it set price averages higher than they actually were. If this were so, it was not hard for some farmers to envisage an alarming sequence of events: incorrectly reported prices above 80s. would lead to open ports, incoming grain, and falling prices. As it happened the year 1818 saw the largest grain imports of any year until that time.[31]

Thus in the latter months of 1818 something like a movement for general protection began to take shape. The December issue of the Edinburgh Magazine noted that the Corn Laws were in disfavor, and that petitions circulating throughout most of the English counties had requested an increased agricultural protection.[32] Local newspapers began to report the progress of the petition. The Kentish Gazette observed that by Christmas, 1818, the signatures of occupiers of 40,000 acres had been collected; and the Suffolk Chronicle wrote that the petition had been received locally "with almost universal cordiality."[33] The Farmers' Journal wrote (probably with some exaggeration) that forty-three counties of England and Wales had taken up the Agricultural

Petition "with promptitude and spirit."[34] Early in December Webb Hall
and the younger Ellman issued a declaration stating the necessity
for committees of management in every county, and for a permanent
committee in Westminster to conduct the county petitions through
parliament. The declaration also announced a meeting for January 14,
1819, to be held at Henderson's Hotel in Westminster "to set this
business in motion."[35]

At this meeting, chaired by Webb Hall, there were thirteen men
present representing nine counties: one each from Berkshire, Devonshire, Herefordshire, Oxfordshire, Sussex, and Warwickshire; two from
Gloucestershire and Essex; and three from Suffolk.[36] The new association took for itself the grandiloquent title of "The Legal and Constitutional Association of Agriculturists, for the Protection of the
Rights and Interests of Agriculture in the United Kingdom of Great
Britain and Ireland." Webb Hall probably chose the title to prevent
the association from being taken for a group of noisy and troublesome
Radicals. The London meeting was certainly unobtrusive enough: there
was so little fanfare that The Times missed it altogether and only
learned of a second meeting in February indirectly from a provincial
newspaper.[37]

Webb Hall's statement, which the meeting (or Central Association
as the London meeting was later called) accepted, had little in it
that was new. The Association would seek an import duty on agricultural products equivalent to taxes and tithes that English farmers
had to pay on their own produce; with such a duty there would be no
need for the mischievous machinery of the averages. Webb Hall and

his supporters paid lip service to free trade and argued that agriculture merely sought the sort of protection already granted to mer-
chants and manufacturers.

After this initial meeting to formulate intentions, the activities of the Central Association are not altogether clear. Apparently
it convened in London for several weeks at a time, with headquarters
at Henderson's Hotel, publishing reports and propaganda at the
Farmers' Journal office, forwarding to parliament the petitions received from the local associations, and communicating with such associations by letter and through the Farmers' Journal. Often enough
it was advice on techniques of organization that was sent down to the
localities, particularly by the resourceful Webb Hall. He recommended
that protectionists carry about printed petitions in small tins which
could fit into their pockets and be readily brought forth at markets
and fairs for prompt signature; that the Farmers' Journal be distributed free to farmers' inns; and that if discouragement seized them
they remember the heartening example of William Wilberforce.[38] Webb
Hall was also assiduous in furnishing the press with news of the associations. His industry in sending details of the Henderson's Hotel
meetings accounts for the fact that many newspapers reported such
meetings fully.[39] Webb Hall well knew the importance of winning the
support of the newspaper editors; in 1818 he had written that "the
press [was] a far more powerful engine than an army, and we must avail
ourselves of its operation if we mean to succeed."[40]

It is also not altogether clear what the local associations did,
or how numerous and large they were.[41] They seem to have adopted an
organization similar to that of the Central Association—a committee

of management, a subscription, and a program based on the Central Association's resolutions. Their chief activity was the circulation
of petitions, the gathering of signatures, and the forwarding of these
signed petitions to the Central Association and ultimately to parliament.

By the end of 1819 twenty English counties had sent representatives to the Central Association;[42] and the Farmers' Journal boasted
that some fifty local associations had been f ormed--"a thing never
heard of before in the world in an agricultural population."[43] The
strength of these associations in their several counties is hard to
assess. They were perhaps most vigorous in Essex, Sussex, Gloucestershire, and Suffolk. But it seems that none grew strong enough to
capture that important vehicle of local politics, the county meeting.[44]
One might infer from the failure to capture the county meeting that
the governing class of the counties--especially the great landed
families--stood aside from the Agricultural Association. Landlords
were, not surprisingly, reluctant to encourage an association which
threatened to organize their tenants in order to promote such an extreme course of action as complete protection. The fact that landlords had not been active in the associations is evident from a contemporary pamphlet in which the writer chastised his fellow landlords.
The author, C.C. Western of Essex, was a noted agricultural improver
and M.P. In his pamphlet Western claimed that the tenants had done
more to save the landlords from ruin than they themselves. The
tenants "have borne the brunt of the storm, they have been far more
exposed to it than we have yet been, they have struggled manfully,
and we have hitherto remained passive, with our hands before us, or

reluctantly followed where they have led--thus reversing the more
natural, and formerly the more usual order of things. . . ."[45] Webb
Hall himself--and perhaps he was merely putting a good face on it--
freely admitted that his movement was not a landowner's movement. Although the radical William Cobbett insisted that the Farmers' Journal
should be called the Landlords' Journal, Webb Hall denied this, argu-
ing that landowners had no real interest in his movement.[46] "[T]he
whole grievance is fixed on the tenant, or more correctly speaking,
on THE CULTIVATORS OF THE SOIL, whether they be owners in fee, for a
term of years, or tenants at will; and for these reasons the cultivators of the soil, and they alone, can become petitioners for redress:
hence in all meetings, correctly styled, the petitioners are called
AGRICULTURISTS, a word which embraces and combines the character of
every owner of every tenure, in possession, which exists. Hence, also,
the title of AGRICULTURAL PETITIONS."[47]

Scrutiny of the personnel of the Central Association and of the
local associations fails to disclose a single member of an important
landed family. If the persons who can be positively identified are
typical of the leadership of the Agricultural Association, it would
seem that its leadership was recruited variously: from
small squires; more frequently from large tenant farmers;
and from the class of men who combined tenant farming with ownership
of some land or with a rural occupation like milling or land agency.
Webb Hall, it has been noted, was a solicitor and tenant farmer and
an extensive grazier. Both the Ellmans were extensive graziers, the
father was an agent as well and an occupier of two farms totalling 1400
acres near Lewes;the son was an occupier of 1200 acres. R.C. Harvey,

chairman of the Harleston (Norfolk) Association, owned two thirds of his 850 acre farm and was also a miller. Job Lousley, a farmer at Blewbury, Berks, and one of the original thirteen at the first Henderson's meeting, occupied 200 acres; he also kept some sheep. Thomas Evans, who became chairman of the Tewksbury (Gloucestershire) Association in 1821, occupied nearly 700 acres of land. John Martyn Bligh, chairman of the Cornwall Association, farmed "a pretty considerable" estate of his own; he was also a land agent, and served as steward for part of the Duchy of Cornwall. John Brickwell, chairman of the Buckingham (town) Association, occupied a farm of 500 acres, 56 of which were his own.[48]

This is not to say that there was no landlord support whatsoever outside the Association. At least one, Lord Sheffield, even claimed to have "zealously promoted" the agricultural associations; in 1819 he wrote Arthur Young that he intended to send to the associations a recent print of his on the necessity for protection. Sheffield thought that the proliferation of the societies would eventually make it possible to induce the government to revise the corn laws.[49] On the whole, however, it seems that members of the associations came from the more independent tenant farmers and small owners, especially those who were wool growers.

When the second meeting of the Central Association was held at Henderson's Hotel on February 15, 1819, attendance had risen from thirteen to thirty-eight and the number of counties represented from nine to seventeen. Webb Hall reported to the meeting that he had sent each member of the cabinet a copy of the resolutions adopted in January.[50] Ten days later, on February 25, a committee of six from

the Central Association, headed by Webb Hall and accompanied by several
members of parliament,[51] had an interview with F.J. Robinson, then
President of the Board of Trade. But Robinson was unmoved by the
protectionist argument and told the delegation that it was inexpedient
to alter the existing laws and that the deepening distress was only
temporary.[52] The government did, however, concede in 1819 an import
duty on wool although it was not as heavy a duty as the Agricultural
Association wanted.

Not until May, 1820, did the Agricultural Association gain a foothold in the Commons. Beginning on May 1, a series of meetings took
place at Henderson's Hotel and for the first time several M.P.'s were
present: C.C. Western, George Holme Sumner, E.J. Curteis, R.D.
Grosvenor, and John Fane.[53] Holme Sumner moved in the House of Commons on July 24 for a select committee on agricultural distress. He
presented 218 protectionist petitions[54] as proof of "the ruinous consequences of a competition with foreigners." In the ensuing parliamentary debate F.J. Robinson spoke for the government. He was as reluctant to take action as he had been a year earlier. Deploring the
Agricultural Associations, he noted that "great pains have been taken
in the agricultural districts to excite a conviction that the existing law for the protection of agriculture was inoperative. Associations were established from one end of the kingdom to the other, for
the purpose of concentrating in one mass the whole of the agricultural
population, in order to bring their case more effectually under the
consideration of Parliament. In addition to this, it was deeply to
be lamented that a kind of manifesto had been issued by an individual,
whose name had been very conspicuous in these transactions, in which

manifesto (for he could call it by no other title) the case of the
agriculturists had been stated with a great deal of culpable exaggeration."[55] For one thing (said Robinson), the manifesto overlooked
the fact that England was just emerging from a war of "unprecedented
duration and singularity"; for another it misled the farmers into
thinking that parliament had at hand some easy remedy for rural distress. Another government economic expert and future President of the
Board of Trade, William Huskisson, concurred: "The evil was to be
remedied only by time."[56]

The long debate drew to a close about four o'clock in the morning.
The consensus of the House had seemed to be against the motion for a
select committee. But to the surprise of everyone Holme Sumner's
motion carried, 150 to 101. The next day, however, the House narrowed
the scope of inquiry from the general subject to agricultural distress
to the particular subject of how the Corn Law averages were derived.
When the committee reported in July, it was too late in the session
for action.

Still, a foothold had been gained. And when distress deepened
late in 1820 and the local associations grew more active, resolutions
and petitions were adopted objecting to the limited scope of the recent parliamentary committee and asking for the appointment of another
committee with full investigating powers. This time the government
complied. Between 1819 and 1821, hundreds of petitions were presented
on the Corn Law of 1815--the greatest number of petitions ever presented to parliament to that time on one subject.[57] Such an outpour-
ing of sentiment made it impossible to delay any longer an inquiry.

The Farmers' Journal congratulated its readers and correspondents; their arguments and perseverance had finally gained a hearing.[58]

The protectionist chairman of the new committee, T.S. Gooch, notified Webb Hall that the Central Association was to provide some witnesses for the committee's hearing. Webb Hall himself, the Ellmans, and others who were connected with the movement testified before the committee.[59] They asked for a fixed duty of 40s. a quarter of wheat and corresponding duties on other agricultural products. One notable member of the committee was David Ricardo, whose reputation as an economist was then at its height. Ricardo saw his role on the committee as one to correct "mistaken principles." As he wrote to a friend: "It was my business to show how little [farmers] were qualified to be advisers on this important question, by exposing their ignorance of the first principles which should guide our judgements."[60] Ricardo did his work only too well: his relentless questions quickly reduced Webb Hall to sorry blustering and finally to abject confessions of ignorance.[61] Webb Hall had not pondered the theory of comparative advantage and he had not been careful about the economic facts on which he founded his opinions. The protectionist rout before the committee was obvious to all. William Jacob, in an extensive memorandum on the committee sittings prepared for Huskisson, summed up contemporary opinion. "Mr. Ellman," wrote Jacob scornfully, "just seems to have been tutored at Henderson's": Ellman's evidence was "the most whimsical...ever exhibited to any legislative body." Jacob was no less severe about Webb Hall's testimony, terming it "rather an harangue than evidence."[62]

When it became obvious that a majority of the committee was opposed to the demands of the protectionists, the protectionist M.P.'s
ceased attending committee meetings in an effort to prevent the report from appearing.[63] This only gave the others a free hand and on
June 18, 1821, the report, credited to Huskisson, was presented. It
rejected the claims of the protectionists that grain prices had been
depressed due to the importations of 1818 and early 1819. The importations had been necessary and had been largely disposed of during
those years and present prices of grain could only be remotely connected with the importations of more than two years past. The committee also rejected the proposal for high protective duties as virtually prohibiting imports. "All we need say of it," wrote the
Farmers' Journal of the report, "is that in its total effect it is
quite in opposition to the prayers of the petitioners."[64]

The report of 1821 marked the beginning of the end of Webb Hall's
movement. Webb Hall's loss of influence was revealed in the 1822
parliamentary session. In January, 1822, Charles W. Wynn, writing to
the Duke of Buckingham had predicted that the House of Commons would
resist any attempt at tampering with the price of corn "notwithstand-
ing the nonsense of Mr. Webb Hall and his petitioners." Wynn thought
that the fallacies of Webb Hall were now too plain and "really too
absurd for even a country gentleman to swallow."[65] Wynn proved correct in his opinion. When Sir Thomas Lethbridge moved the adoption
of the protectionist program during the debates on the third report
on agricultural distress in May, 1822, the motion was overwhelmingly
defeated (23-243).[66] Webb Hall's parliamentary support had dwindled
away.

Meanwhile Webb Hall was losing support of the press in the countryside. Naturally he had detractors from the start. Most vociferous
was the whiggish Alfred, published at Exeter, which favored free trade.
In March, 1821, the Alfred deplored that Webb Hall's "trash and nonsense" had been accepted by a large proportion of the country.[67]
Webb Hall's testimony in 1821 before the committee on the state of
agriculture gave the Alfred more ammunition. Terming him a "puff-ball
of vanity and ignorance," the Alfred savagely attacked Webb Hall's
weakness in political economy.[68] More harmful to Webb Hall was the
loss of former supporters, such as the Bristol Observer. In 1819,
the editor of the Observer based his support for protection upon the
belief that imports of agricultural products would ruin English
farmers thus destroying an extensive market for English manufacturers.[69]
From 1819 through 1821, the Observer continued its support for agricultural protection. By mid-1822, however, the Observer was becoming
critical of Webb Hall. It thought the 40s. a quarter duty he demanded
was too high, and charged the agricultural advocates with "a mystifi-
cation of their case of late."[70] Thereafter, articles sympathetic to
the agriculturists disappeared from the Observer's columns.

In accounting for the decline of the Agricultural Association,
one must recognize that it suffered from severe competition; it was
not the only voice to be heard proposing relief for rural distress.
As early as February, 1820, Thomas Attwood, a Birmingham banker, was
seeking a rural hearing for his inflationary schemes by writing to
the Farmers' Journal.[71] Soon Attwood and Webb Hall were engaged in
controversy in the pages of the Journal; Attwood maintained that
Peel's Act of 1819 was the cause of the distress while Webb Hall

insisted that agricultural importations were the cause.[72] Webb Hall
was concerned lest the currency question divert the attention of the
movement from its protectionist goal, and in May of 1820, the Central
Association announced its determination not to consider the subject.[73]
As early as the summer of 1820, the _Farmers' Journal_ was warming to
Attwood's ideas: "[In] truth, the more the Ministry set their faces
against duties on foreign corn, the more necessary it becomes to view
the other mode of relief with anxiety and hope."[74] R.C. Harvey, one
of Webb Hall's lieutenants, plainly revealed in his evidence before the
Agricultural Committee of 1821 that he also had come under Attwood's
influence.[75] Some of the agricultural associations which met in the
latter half of 1821 revealed a similar distraction.[76]

A further problem for the protectionist movement was the division
of interest among the agriculturists themselves. Stock farmers could
hardly look with enthusiasm upon a plan which seemed certain to raise
the price of all grains--including feed grains. Nor was there unanimity
among arable farmers. At a meeting of owners and occupiers of western
Kent in April, 1820, there was evidence of a conflict between corn and
hop growers. The meetings had been called to consider what steps
should be taken to relieve the agricultural distress; a committee was
appointed to attend the Henderson's Hotel meetings and a petition
drawn up. A Mr. Winch of Hawkhurst said that he had not heard the
petition mention hop farmers. Although assured by others at the meeting that it did, he remained unconvinced. Winch said that near him
lived numerous farmers whose principal crop was hops, and who grew
little corn. Therefore, "in his part of the country, the high price
of corn could be of no benefit to the farmers. They did not grow

enough to make it an object, and he believed, that where one man would gain by the high price of corn, twenty would be hurt by it."[77] It was finally decided to send a petition which did not name any specific grievance and was to speak rather in general terms of the distress.

The most challenging opposition to Webb Hall's protectionist movement came from two very different sources--William Cobbett and the aristocratic Whig families of the countryside. Both Cobbett and the Whigs recognized that profitable fishing might be found in the troubled waters of agricultural distress. Unlike Webb Hall they both advocated retrenchment and parliamentary reform as the solution to the problems facing farmers. In addition Cobbett spoke against Peel's Act and advocated what he called an "equitable adjustment" of farmers' burdens. Cobbett's championing of the farmers was consistent with his long career of public agitation. For the Whigs there was a hope that some political benefit might be reaped against the Tory government then in power. Webb Hall could have made little headway against the eloquence of Cobbett, or the powerful force of local Whig influence. This will be examined in more detail in the following chapter.

In spite of the decline of his influence, Webb Hall was far from idle or reduced to despair. When the Board of Agriculture held its second annual cattle show in April, 1822, Webb Hall turned it into a protectionist meeting.[78] Then in December he was active once again at Henderson's Hotel when a fund of £421 was collected.[79] Little response, however, now came from the countryside for a protectionist program. Agricultural prices were beginning to rise and by mid-1823 farmers were losing interest in politics and agitation. Webb Hall

made his last public appearance in December, 1823, when he judged livestock at the Bath and West Society's show. Two months later he was
dead of tetanus occasioned by a fall from his horse.

Webb Hall's death marked the end of an important episode in the
story of agricultural organization and agitation. A rural public
opinion had come to life under the impact of agricultural depression.
Although the Agricultural Association failed, it set a precedent for
future farmers' organizations on a national scale, and it helped to
arouse a debate on the state of agriculture which was to be carried on
for at least another quarter of a century.

48

Footnotes, Chapter II

[1] An earlier version of this chapter by David Spring and Travis L. Crosby appeared in The Jnl. of British Studies, Vol. I, Vol. I, no. 1 (Nov. 1962), pp. 115-31. I'm very grateful to the editors of the JBS for allowing me to include it here.

[2] The growing importance of American grain in the English market (before strained relations in 1810 lessened it) is noted in William F. Galpin, The Grain Supply of England during the Napoleonic Period (New York, 1925), Chap. VIII "Anglo-American Grain Trade 1800-1813".

[3] Farmers Jnl., Jan. 9, 1815.

[4] Ibid.

[5] Ibid., January 16, 1815.

[6] Stamford Mercury, Feb. 3, 1815.

[7] Norfolk Chr., Jan. 21, 1815.

[8] Hereford Jnl., Feb. 22, 1815.

[9] Jnls. H. of L., vol. XL (1815).

[10] P.R.O., H.O./142.

[11] Farmers' Jnl., Jan. 29, 1816.

[12] The letter was dated Oct. 20, 1819; quoted in Mitchison, "The Old Board of Agriculture, 1793-1822," Eng. Hist. Rev., p. 64. The reference was to the radical agitator, Henry Hunt.

[13] R. Robson, The Attorney in Eighteenth-Century England (Cambridge, 1959), passim.

[14] Gentleman's Magazine, Vol. XCIV (1824), pp. 464-65. Other sources of this biographical sketch are Farmers' Jnl., Annual Statement, 1825; and Bristol Jnl., Feb. 23, 1824.

[15] Gentleman's Magazine, Vol. XCIV (1824), p. 465; Farmers' Jnl., Mar. 20, 1820.

[16] The fine-wooled Merino had only recently been introduced to English agriculture. George III, Lord Somerville, and others were assiduous in their efforts to establish them in England. Brief sketches of the Merino experiment are in E. Lipson, A Short History of Wool and its Manufacture (London, 1953), esp. Chap. III, "Merino and Cross-bred Wool"; and Robert Trow-Smith, A History of the British Livestock Industry, 1700-1900 (London, 1959), pp. 151 ff. and passim.

[17] Farmers' Jnl., Annual Statement, 1824.

[18] "On the Trade in Wool and Woollens including an Exposition of the Commercial Situation of the British Empire," Pamphleteer, Vol. III, no. 6 (1814), pp. 325-26.

[19] Sir Ernest Clarke, History of the Board of Agriculture 1793-1833 (London, 1898), p. 40; "Transactions of the Bath and West of England Society," Vol. VIII, p. 215. The "Transactions" are in manuscript in the library of the Bath and West of England Society at Bath.

[20] Farmers' Jnl., Feb. 5, 1816.

[21] Ibid.

[22] Other products mentioned specifically were: meal, flour, rye, oats, pease, beans, barley, beer or bigg, flax, hemp, hides, tallow, seeds, butter, and cheese. The resolutions are in Farmers' Jnl., Mar. 25, 1816.

[23] Farmers' Jnl., Mar. 11, 1816.

[24] William Smart, Economic Annals of the Nineteenth Century, Vol. I, pp. 489-90. Of course, to use wheat prices as a measure of prosperity is too easy a generalization, but it can perhaps indicate a trend among the larger arable farmers. A recent statement on this is found in A.H. John, "The Course of Agricultural Change 1660-1760," in L.S. Pressnell (ed.), Studies in the Industrial Revolution (London, 1960), pp. 125-55.

[25] The following is a table of wool prices for the years with which this chapter is concerned. The prices are given in pence per pound:

Year	Merino	Southdown	Kent Long
1815	--	24	22
1816	30	17.6	14
1817	24	19.5	15
1818	27	25.2	24
1819	20	22.2	15
1820	20	17	16
1821	18	15.1	13

Year	Merino	Southdown	Kent Long
1822	18	14	11
1823	15	15	12
1824	21	13	13

The merino price scale is taken from the House of Lords' Report on British Wool Trade, 1828 (Evidence of George Webb Hall, Jr.), quoted in James Bischoff, A Comprehensive History of the Woollen and Worsted Manufacturers (London, 1842), Vol. II, p. 126. Southdown and Kent Long wool prices are from A.D. Gayer, W.W. Rostow, and A.J. Schwartz, The Growth and Fluctuation of the British Economy 1780-1850 (Oxford, 1953), Vol. I, pp. 155, 199.

[26] H. Heaton, The Yorkshire Woollen and Worsted Industries (Oxford, 1920), pp. 325-6.

[27] First Report of the Select Committee on Seeds and Wools, Parliamentary Papers (1816), Vol. I.

[28] Farmers' Jnl., Aug. 5, and Aug. 12, 1816.

[29] Ibid., Oct. 14, 1816. Ellman later explained that since there was no permanent association of this type in Sussex, he had been invited to join the Gloucester and Somerset Association (Farmers' Jnl., Jan. 27, 1817).

[30] Farmers' Jnl., May 5, 1817.

[31] Barnes, A History of the English Corn Laws, p. 162.

[32] Quoted in Smart, Economic Annals, Vol. I, p. 654.

[33]Kentish Gaz., Dec. 25 and 29, 1818; Suffolk Chr., Dec. 12, 1818, and Jan. 9, 1819.

[34]Farmers' Jnl., Dec. 28, 1818.

[35]Ibid., Dec. 7, 1818.

[36]The Origin and Proceedings of the Agricultural Associations in Great Britain (London, n.d.); Farmers' Jnl., Jan. 18, 1819.

[37]The Times, Feb. 24, 1819.

[38]Farmers' Jnl., Jan. 25, 1819, Apr. 12, 1819, and July 26, 1819. These recommendations were made over the signature of "Alpha", Webb Hall's pseudonym for writing in the Farmers' Journal.

[39]The Norwich Courier (June 3, 1820), in commenting on a pamphlet sent to it by Webb Hall, observed that copies also had been sent to all M.P.'s and to "every Editor of a newspaper throughout the kingdom."

[40]Farmers' Jnl., Nov. 16, 1818.

[41]Some attendance figures were recorded in the Farmers' Jnl.; for example, the smallest attendance (seventeen) was at Henley on Thames, Oxford, reported in the April 19, 1819 issue; the largest was a meeting at Ilsey, Berks (Farmers' Jnl., May 24, 1819), where sixty were present. Of other attendance figures given, most seem to fall between twenty-five and thirty-five.

[42]These counties were: Gloucestershire, Bedfordshire, Berkshire, Cambridgeshire, Essex, Hampshire, Herefordshire, Hertfordshire, Huntingdonshire, Middlesex, Norfolk, Oxfordshire, Staffordshire, Suffolk, Surrey, Sussex, Warwickshire, Cornwall, Northamptonshire, and Devonshire; see The Origin and Proceedings of the Agricultural Associations in Great Britain.

[43]Farmers' Jnl., Dec. 6, 1819. One hundred associations were claimed in October, 1820 (Farmers' Jnl., Oct. 30, 1820).

[44]Although Halévy takes notice of Webb Hall, his observation that county meetings were important in the movement is incorrect (Halévy, History, Vol. II, p. 110).

[45]C.C. Western, Address to the Land Owners of the United Empire (London, 1822), p. 4.

[46]Cobbett's Weekly Political Register, Vol. XXXIX, no. 4, p. 274.

[47]Farmers' Jnl., May 3, 1819.

[48]Information on these farmers is found scattered in a series of Parliamentary Reports, including Report on the State of Agriculture, Parliamentary Papers (1820), Vol. II; Report on the State of Agriculture, Parliamentary Papers (1821), Vol. IX; and Second Report on the State of Agriculture, Parliamentary Papers (1836), Vol. VIII.

[49]Young Papers, Add. MSS 35133, ff. 439 and 467, Sheffield to Arthur Young.

[50]Farmers' Jnl., Jan. 25, 1819.

[51]C.C. Western, Charles Dundas, John Fane, Sir Charles Monck, William Dickinson.

[52]Farmers' Jnl., Mar. 8, 1819. Lord Liverpool was of the same opinion; he thought the farmers were exaggerating. In a letter to Wellington dated Sept. 12, 1819, he reported his observations of a recent tour. Although Lancashire was distressed; "the condition of almost every other part of the country is satisfactory; poor-rates are falling, crimes are diminishing, and the agricultural counties are in a state of progressive prosperity. . . ." Despatches, Correspondence, and Memoranda of Field Marshall Arthur Duke of Wellington, ed. Duke of Wellington (London, 1867), Vol. I, p. 76.

[53]Farmers' Jnl., May 8, 1820. Another opportunity for the protection-ists to discuss their strategy was at the spring Merino show held in mid-May. In attendance were Webb Hall, Holme Sumner, Fane, and Western (Farmers' Jnl., May 15, 1820). Western was a noted Merino grower and frequently chaired the Merino show meetings.

[54]Farmers' Jnl., July 24, 1820.

[55]Hansard, 2nd Ser., Vol. I, 642.

[56]Ibid., 631.

[57]Smart, Economic Annals, Vol. II, p. 3 claims that 1200 petitions were presented, but this is probably too high an estimate. Reports from Committees, Parliamentary Papers (1822), V, lists the origins of all petitions on the subject of agricultural distress from 1820 to March, 1822. There were 159 presented in 1820, 187 in 1821, and 129 for the first five months of 1822.

[58]Farmers' Jnl., Mar. 12, 1821.

[59]For Webb Hall's testimony, see Report on the State of Agriculture, Parliamentary Papers (1821), Vol. IX, pp. 163ff.

[60]P. Sraffa (ed.), The Works and Correspondence of David Ricardo (Cambridge, 1952), Vol. VIII, pp. 369-70.

[61]See especially pp. 165, 168-69, and 174 of the Report.

[62]Huskisson Papers, Add. MSS 38742, ff. 230-31. Jacob, who had been M.P. for Rye from 1808-1812, was a merchant with connections in South America. He later served as comptroller of corn returns to the Board of Trade (DNB).

[63]Smart, Economic Annals, Vol. II, p. 6, note 2; and K.G. Feiling, The Second Tory Party, 1714-1832 (London, 1951), p. 322.

[64]Farmers' Jnl., June 25, 1821.

[65]Duke of Buckingham and Chandos, Memoirs of the Court of George IV, 1820-30 (London, 1850), Vol. I, pp. 276-280.

[66]Hansard, 2nd Ser., Vol. VII, 403-4.

[67]The Alfred, Mar. 13, 1821.

[68]Ibid., Apr. 10, 1821.

[69]Bristol Obs., Nov. 18, 1819.

[70]Ibid., May 22, 1820.

[71]See C.M. Wakefield, The Life of Thomas Attwood (London, 1885), passim.

[72]The Journal summarizes the views of the combatants thus: "It is said of Mr. Attwood, that he is all cash, and of Mr. Webb Hall that he is all corn" (Farmers' Jnl., Feb. 21, 1820).

[73]Farmers' Jnl., May 8, 1820.

[74]Ibid., June 26, 1820.

[75]Report on the State of Agriculture, Parliamentary Papers (1821), Vol. IX, p. 35.

[76]See for example, the reports of the South Bucks Agricultural Association (Farmers' Jnl., Aug. 27, 1821); the Worcestershire Agricultural Association (Farmers' Jnl., Sept. 17, 1821); and the Stow-on-the-Wold (Gloucestershire) Agricultural Association (Farmers' Jnl., Dec. 6, 1821).

[77]See the account in the Kentish Gaz., Apr. 25, 1820.

[78]Farmers' Jnl., Apr. 29, 1822.

[79]Ibid., Aug. 4, 1823.

Chapter III--The Farmer as Reformer

Farmers' search for a solution to agricultural depression found
its most radical form in the early 1820's in a series of county meetings
promoted by parliamentary reformers. We have already observed that the
easing of attendance restrictions at county meetings tended to make
them a more open forum, permitting even landless tenant farmers to attend. The loosening of attendance restriction at county meetings brought
about a loss of control by wielders of local influence. The effect was
to expose the meetings to the demagogic appeals of Radical agitators,
the most notable of whom was William Cobbett. Cobbett's strong (and
changeable) opinions, expressed in a lucid and didactic prose, gave
him a wide readership throughout the whole of England; and his homely
appearance, rural upbringing, and knowledge of country matters gave
him special claims upon the attention of the distressed farmers in the
early 1820's.[1]

In common with other Radicals, Cobbett believed that parliament had
to be reformed. He made a direct connection between an unreformed
parliament and the agricultural depression. Cobbett maintained that
the cause of the depression was the government's policy of narrowing
the once plentiful issues of paper money--a policy culminating in Peel's
Act of 1819. More specifically, he argued that the deflationary effect
of Peel's Act was the cause of the low agricultural prices and would
drive them still lower. The falling agricultural prices put the farmer
in an especially bad position with his fixed tithes, rates, and taxes.

Since the existing House of Commons would not give the agriculturist the
relief he needed--either a repeal of Peel's Act or a reduction of taxes--
then it must be reformed.

In 1821 Cobbett launched a country campaign to convince farmers of
his view of the distress. In his Political Register he issued a special
"New Year's Gift to Farmers," followed by a political address "To Farmers'
Wives." In January, 1822, he collected some of his writings into a
pamphlet, "The Farmers' Friend"; this was followed in March by "The
Farmers' Wive's Friend." Cobbett also supplemented these political
prints with others purely agricultural; among them were practical
farming hints in the Register, his Cottage Economy, and his edition
of Jethro Tull's Husbandry.[2]

Cobbett's most effective method of persuasion was his frequent
appearance about the countryside as he spoke to farmers at their market dinners, fairs, and most importantly at country meetings. While
planning a part of his itinerary in September, 1822, Cobbett wrote of
his intention: "I am going to place myself. . .in the midst of the
great fairs of the west, in order before the winter campaign begins,
that I may see as many farmers as possible, and that they may hear my
opinions, and I theirs."[3] Thus began Cobbett's famous rural rides.

The first important meeting that Cobbett attended in his country campaign was at Battle, Sussex, in January, 1822. There, a meeting had been
called by landlords and farmers to discuss a petition on the agricultural distress. The three hundred in attendance chose Lord Ashburnham
as chairman. E.J. Curteis, M.P. for Sussex, opened the meeting with a
speech which painted in dark colors the condition of the agriculturists.

He was followed by Cobbett, whose remarks were directed against Webb
Hall and his protectionist movement. He denied that a new Corn Bill
would benefit agriculturists. In speaking against "the crude notions
of Mr. Webb Hall," Cobbett maintained that imports of foreign grain had
nothing to do with the distress. He then concluded with a general attack on Peel's Act.[4]

By the end of 1822 Cobbett was a regular feature at the markets
and fairs of rural England. The following itinerary gives some idea
of how widely Cobbett traveled.[5] On September 28, 1822, he dined and
spoke in the Swan Inn with the farmers who had come to Winchester market day. Then, after visiting the Weyhill fair, he spent some days at
Andover speaking with farmers. On October 17, Cobbett left Hampshire
and went into Berkshire. Five days later Cobbett went into Wiltshire
and spoke to some five hundred farmers at Salisbury. On November 9,
Cobbett returned to Berkshire and noted of a meeting held there: "This
has been a fine meeting at Reading! I feel very proud of it."[6]

Cobbett had reason to be pleased. The more influence Webb Hall
lost among the farmers, the more Cobbett gained. As early as January,
1822, the Worcester Journal noted: "The opinion that the present
distress among the Agriculturists is, to a degree at least, occasioned
by a too sudden resumption of cash payments, appears to be gaining
ground, and the assertion that the importation of foreign corn is the
chief cause of the distress, is losing ground."[7] Even those who did
not really agree with Cobbett's views were sometimes carried by the
vigor of his presentation. The Bristol Observer, in commenting on
"this ubiquitary freeholder", noted Cobbett's success: "A good dinner
and a bottle of wine for twelve shillings, and Mr. Cobbett 'free,

gratis, and all for nothing,' are indeed powerful attractions,---no wonder that the Farmers are glad to drown their cares in wine and oratory on such easy terms."[8]

No less active than Cobbett in the countryside were the Whigs. In adopting reform as a party platform, the Whigs hoped to buttress their weakened party, undermined during the Napoleonic Wars by internal divisions and uncertain leadership. The successful conclusion of the wars by Lord Liverpool's Tory government placed the Whigs at a further disadvantage. In the years after 1815, therefore, the Whigs sought political footholds where they could be found. Agricultural depression provided an ideal opportunity. By exploiting rural disaffection, the Whigs hoped to gain country support for their program of moderate parliamentary reform and economic retrenchment. That the Whig cry of retrenchment would find a reception among farmers was evident from their increasing impatience with the special agricultural taxes. Reform, however, posed a more difficult problem. The Whigs had to be circumspect in advocating reform--fervent enough to draw the teeth of more radical advocates yet moderate enough to prevent alarm among Whig country squires and the manufacturing interest of the industrial north.

By August, 1819, the Whigs were ready to begin an active program for parliamentary reform: events favored a positive stand. Reform agitation by unemployed urban working classes had culminated in a meeting of thousands at St. Peter's Fields, Manchester, on August 16, 1819, to hear the Radical Henry Hunt speak. When local magistrates called in regular cavalry to disperse the crowd, a struggle followed in which eleven were killed and over 400 wounded. Thus was "Peterloo" added to the reform canon. In a letter to Henry Brougham a few days after

Peterloo, the Whig leader Lord Grey wrote that "everything is tending, and has been for some time tending, to a complete separation between the higher and lower orders of society; a state of things which can only end in the destruction of liberty, or in a convulsion which may too probably produce the same result. It has sometimes occurred to me that we ought to try once more whether, by placing ourselves on the middle ground, condemning the conduct of Hunt and his associates, but strenuously resisting the attempt that is making to attack through them the safe-guards of the constitution, we could not rally to our standard all moderate and reasonable men (and a great portion of the property of the country), to whom the people might again be brought to look at as their natural leaders and protectors."[9] Whig intentions to capitalize on Peterloo were indicated by Earl Fitzwilliam's chairing of the Yorkshire county meetings to protest against Peterloo, and by Lord John Russell's Grampound disfranchisement speech in December, 1819. The Whigs were exhibiting themselves as champions of the popular cause and thus (in Lord John Russell's words) "renewing the old and natural alliance between the Whigs and the people and weakening the influence of the Radicals with the latter."[10]

By the beginning of 1821 the Whigs decided to expand the ranks of the reformers by actively campaigning in the country. Creevy, the Whig diarist, voiced the sentiments of many Whig reformers when he wrote that if the distress would "but pinch these dirty, shabby landed voters two sessions more, there's no saying at what degree of purity we shall arrive."[11] Methods adopted by the Whigs to promote reform in the countryside were diverse, but the principle--exertion by Whig landlords of their influence upon local gentry and agriculturists--was unvarying.

This often took the form of sponsoring local meetings. For example, a series of meetings of the Norfolk and Suffolk hundreds was held in the spring of 1822. The object of the meetings was to provide a channel whereby Whig-inspired strictures on the government could reach parliament through the traditional method of petitions. As that staunch Whig, Coke of Norfolk, observed: hundred meetings were useful "because it was so teasing to Ministers to have petition after petition presented." Indeed, "his great object was to plague the Ministers from morning to night. If they (the Hundred meetings) did but supply him with Petitions he would attend to present one every day."[12] Thus by meeting in hundreds the Whigs could harass the government more effectively; only one petition could be sent from a county meeting, but if every hundred of a county met, the number of petitions would be greatly increased (Norfolk alone had thirty-three hundreds). A further advantage of hundred meetings was that they were easier to control. An indifferent or anti-reform agriculturist would more likely be overawed at a hundred meeting by an illustrious Whig presence than at a county meeting where anonymous thousands were present. Attendance at the meetings might vary from fifty--as at the Humbleyard, Norfolk, meeting-- to five hundred, as at North Erpingham, Norfolk.[13] But most meetings had from one to two hundred present.

Although useful to the Whigs, the hundred meetings lacked the respectability of the more traditional county meeting. Therefore the Whigs were no less active in summoning county meetings. A clue to Whig intentions regarding county meetings was given at the Suffolk Fox Dinner at Ipswich in February, 1821. The Earl of Albemarle, who was the principal speaker, praised county meetings as an effective means of demonstrating reform sentiment. County meetings, said Albermarle in a speech redolent of Whiggery, were places where men could form themselves into "a determined and united band for the establishment of rational and constitutional liberty."[14]

In fact, the month prior to Albemarle's speech had already witnessed a Whig success at a county meeting. At an Oxfordshire county meeting in January, 1821, called to vote a loyal address to the king, Lord Jersey and Lord Holland (who had set off at four in the morning to be with Jersey)[15] turned the meeting to Whig advantage. An amendment to the loyal address moved by Jersey requested that agricultural distress be taken into consideration by the government. "Ministers might not be able to remove the evil altogether," said Jersey, 'but they might pay some attention to the petitions presented on the subject, and they might adopt measures of retrenchment."[16] In the same month at a Kent county meeting Lord Darnley and the Earl of Thanet spread the Whig message of moderate reform. Darnley told the assembly that "if the country could be saved, it must be the Whig aristocracy, who utterly disclaimed all subserviency to the Court or to the mob."[17]

Indeed, the Whig aristocracy took the lead in assiduously cultivating rural opinion. Representatives of important Whig families who were active included: the Earl of Albermarle and Lord Suffield at a January, 1822, Norfolk meeting; Earl Fortescue at a February, 1822, Devonshire meeting; Lord King at the two February, 1822, Surrey meetings; the Duke of Grafton at the Suffolk meetings of March, 1821, and January, 1822; Earl Fitzwilliam and Lord Dacre at a January, 1821, Cambridgeshire meeting; and Lord Milton at a March, 1821, Huntingdonshire meeting.[18] The house of Russell was especially active. The

Marquis of Tavistock was at the Bedfordshire meetings of January, 1821,
and April, 1822; and at the Cambridgeshire meeting of March, 1821.
Lord John Russell attended the Bedfordshire meeting of January, 1821,
and the Huntingdonshire meeting of March, 1821. The Duke of Bedford
wrote and spoke widely in the Whig campaign, and his reputation as an
agriculturist assured a respectful hearing. He spoke at the Cambridge
meetings of March, 1821, and April, 1822, and at the Bedfordshire
meetings of January, 1821, and April, 1822.[19] When unable to attend,
he sometimes wrote letters of instructions to county meetings. To a
Devonshire meeting of February, 1822, he urged the usual retrenchment
and reform, but he also cautioned against protectionism terming it
"that delusive mode of relief which has been so much insisted upon."
He castigated protecting duties as "a project...utterly inconsistent
with sound policy"; but he was thankful to note that the more enlightened
farmers were "opening their eyes to the fallacy of it."[20]

In deciding to promote county meetings, the Whigs risked coming
into open conflict with the Radical agitators. As long as specific
programs for reform remained vague, however, the Whigs and Radicals
could form a tenuous alliance. Against this reformist front the Tories
could not mount an effective counterattack, although there were some
attempts to do so. To detract from the "respectability" (and hence
the influence) of a county meeting, government supporters
could absent themselves. But this sometimes resulted in an uncon-
tested victory for the Whig program and if the absentee were an M.P.,
perhaps even an unanswered attack upon his parliamentary record. For
example, at a January, 1822, Norfolk meeting, Edmund Wodehouse, county
M.P., was censured for deceiving his constituents because, having

voted against the malt duties, he then voted for the government budget.[21]
If, on the other hand, government supporters attended the county meetings they ran the risk of open and obvious defeat. For example, the
attendance of Charles Chaplin, the Tory M.P. for Lincolnshire, at a
Lincolnshire county meeting in late April, 1822, not only resulted in
his defeat by the reformers; his presence removed any stigma of ir-
respectability that might have been brought against the meeting and gave
the impression that the county had been fairly represented by both
sides (as, indeed, it had been).[22] Whiggish Sir Robert Heron, who had
spoken for reform at the meeting, wrote later of it: "We should have
been called a mere rabble had not Chaplin and his friends, amongst
whom were squires and clergy, rather unwisely attended."[23]

That Cobbett's harangues and the Whig country influence were having their effect upon the agriculturists was widely observed. "The
cry of Reform," noted one newspaper, "which was once so rife in the
manufacturing, is now transferred to the agricultural districts."[24]
And as a Lancashire correspondent wrote to Lord Suffield in February,
1822: "Heads are at work and hearts are warming amonst a description
of people who had hitherto thought but lightly of the cause of freedom,
we mean the farmers."[25] The startling development of a reformist trend
among farmers was not to everyone's liking. Some were fearful that
farmers were adopting increasingly Radical attitudes. At least one
member of the Tory government, Huskisson, pondered the menace of
Radicalism and its effect upon the countryside. In a "private and
confidential" letter to Arbuthnot, Huskisson warned that "we must not
shut our Eyes to the Spirit which is spreading through the Country,
even in the agricultural districts."[26] He feared that "the present

straightened circumstances of the yeomanry contrasted with the ease
which they enjoyed during the war" was inclining them to Radicalism.
"Whilst this is the state of the yeomanry, the infection of Radicalism,
which is prevalent in the towns is gradually making its way into the
country." To Huskisson, this was all the more serious because it was
to the yeomanry that the government should look for its salvation: "in
my opinion the period may not be remote, in which we may find it necessary to do something to secure the affection and more cordial good will
of some great class in the state. To bid for the lower classes or the
Manufacturing Population is out of the question. Duty and Policy would
equally forbid it; but the yeomanry are still within our reach, and to
them. . .we must look."

The rise of a Radical spirit among farmers was also charted by
the provincial press. In January, 1822 the Tory Bristol Journal observed that recent rural reform meetings were actually superfluous
since parliament, composed mainly of landowners, would always give a
sympathetic ear to farmers. Such meetings as had been held could become what the Journal called "arenas for faction," or "nurseries for
disaffection." The Journal believed it, therefore, "a serious evil,
that the yeomanry, whose loyalty was in all times exemplary, should
have their minds soured and alienated by inflammatory harangues."[27]
The Times, too, detected a tendency toward agrarian Radicalism and
suggested that "moderate counsels and temperate measures emanating
from persons of dignified station" would be the best method "of ar-
resting the suffering agriculturists in their road to jacobinism."[28]

A Kent county meeting in June, 1822, gave point to The Times' concern, for Cobbett there put forward his Radical ideas at the expense of
the more moderate Whigs. The meeting had been convened by a requisition
signed by several Kentish Whigs as well as numerous owners and occupiers
of land who had previously been ministerial supporters.[29] The meeting
favored reform, but Cobbett's proposal--the abolition of the national
debt to reduce government expenditure and taxes immediately--went far
beyond what the other speakers had advocated. Yet Cobbett's resolution was accepted by the meeting. In a direct contest with leading
Kentish Whigs, Cobbett had emerged the victor. The Norwich Courier,
which claimed that the majority present were not freeholders, called
the resolution "villainous".[30] The Bristol Observer thought "that such
a fellow as Cobbett. . .should be able, in a Meeting called by the
leading Whigs of a rich and respectable county, to stand up and carry
a motion for national bankruptcy, is indeed. . .disgraceful to the said
Patrician Whigs, and to all who were present at the Meeting. . . ."[31]

Cobbett's greatest single success at a county meeting occurred
in Norfolk in January, 1823. His selection of the Norfolk county meeting to propose a detailed radical plan for agricultural relief was
shrewd. Not only would he face the leading Whigs of the county as in
Kent, but also the most respected Whig agriculturist--Coke of Norfolk.
A victory by Cobbett over Coke in his home county could well give an
irresistable impulse to Cobbett's reform program among the distressed
agriculturists.

A large and respectable gathering met in Norwich for the county
meeting on January 3, 1823.[32] Early in the meeting a portentous note
was struck by a Mr. George Watson. He complained of the inactivity

of the great landowners in aiding the tenantry: "I am sorry. . .to
think that they would allow their tenantry to sink into beggary, and
wretchedness without making a single effort on their behalf." Shortly
afterward, Cobbett spoke to the expectant crowd; he moved a twofold
proposal. The first part asked for abolition of sinecures; reduction
of the standing army; the equitable adjustment of private debts; and
the application of church property and crown lands to the liquidation
of the national debt. The second part was calculated to appeal more
directly to the agriculturists. It asked for a one year's suspension
of all distraints for rent; a one year's suspension of all tithe payments; a similar suspension on all processes arising out of mortgage,
bond, annuity, or other contracts affecting houses or land; and the
repeal of all malt, hop, soap, leather, and candle taxes.

Cobbett's proposal was read in the midst of a "tremendous clamour"
as Cobbett's friends and enemies made their sentiments known. When it
was put to a vote, according to the Norfolk Chronicle, Cobbett "shouted
most boisterously, and waving triumphantly in the air both his hands,
in the left of which he tightly clenched a copy of his petition, drew
forth the strangest mixture of applause, yells, groans, and hisses,
that ever were heard at public, or indeed any meeting." There was a
three to one majority in favor of Cobbett's resolution. The county
leaders tried to reverse the vote. Condemning Cobbett's attack upon
the church, the Rev. G. Glover "implored the yeomanry of Norfolk to
come forward, and by rejecting the petition now proposed, rescue their
characters, and the character of the country from the ignominy which
would attach to it by the adoption of so disgraceful a document as
that proposed by Mr. Cobbett." Coke then attempted to save the meeting

for the Whigs by suggesting the petition be read again because (said
Coke) "he really believed that neither the resolutions or the amendment had been sufficiently heard. . .to enable them to form a correct
opinion of their contents." But Coke's attempt to rescind Cobbett's
amendment resulted in a worse defeat for the Whigs--the second vote was
a reported twenty to one majority for Cobbett. Thus Cobbett's Radical
petition was adopted as the official address to parliament from the
county of Norfolk.

The result of the meeting caused a national stir. The Whigs were
humiliated. Coke was convinced that Cobbett had been paid by the
government to discredit them. To a friend, he wrote: "That old vaga-
bond, I am satisfied, is in the pay of the Government, and has been
rewarded for that day's iniquity."[33] Lord Suffield did not seek to
make excuses; he wrote plainly: "We were noodled by old Cobbett! The
Reformers or Patriots are themselves gulled--the Tories triumph and the
nation laughs."[34] Some Radicals were puzzled at the results of the
meeting. Ricardo, in a letter to James Mill, wrote: "Mr. Coke and
Mr. Wodehouse must be very much mortified at the success of Cobbett at
their Norfolk meeting. I confess I am astonished by it. It reflects
no great honour on the assembly to pass such resolutions, and will be
used as an argument by Anti-reformers against the extension of the
suffrage."[35] Some Tories were gratified; Lord Eldon wrote to Lady
F.J. Bankes: "You will see, in this morning's paper, the account of
the meeting in St. Andrew's Hall, Norwich. Mr. Coke and the party had,
acting properly, confined the purpose of the meeting to petition Parliament upon agricultural distress,--when in comes Master Cobbett, and
carries all before him, to petition against a corrupt House of Commons,

for Reform. Coke, Rev. Mr. Glover, etc., all turned into cyphers--as
men of this description always will be when they are such fools as to
suppose that they, riding in a whirlwind, will be suffered to govern
the storm they excite."[36]

The general sensation caused by the Norfolk meeting was reflected
in the attention given it by the press. The Times, after asking what
should be done with the Norfolk petition, gave a straightforward
answer: "Why, spit upon it: first for its stupid malignity, and
next on account of the character of its author."[37] The provincial
press manifested more bewilderment. The Worcester Journal seemed in-
credulous that Coke had been deserted by the farmers of his own county.[38]
The Bury Post thought the meeting "wholly unprecedented." It had a
word of caution for the agriculturists: "Whether or not a considerable
portion of the agriculturists, in their admiration of certain talents
which he possesses, have forgotten the character of Mr. Cobbett. . .we
are ignorant; but we cannot suppose that the great of the farming
interest will be reconciled to the idea of having been led blindfold
by a stranger, and we know not how they can feel secure from his intrusion at a future opportunity."[39]

The Norfolk county meeting of January, 1823, was the high tide of
rural reform sentiment.[40] A meeting composed of a large number of
respectable Norfolk agriculturists had given their approval to a program of radical reform advocated by a popular agitator. The result
of the meeting would have caused considerably less public furor had
the meeting been composed of convinced Radical reformers who would
naturally have supported Cobbett. But general comment after the event
indicated neither that the Norfolk freeholders and farmers were

under-represented nor that the Norwich urban classes had gained
control of it.

Several reasons might be advanced to explain this temporary rad-
icalizing of Norfolk agriculturists. First, as we have seen, there
was a growing spirit of reform among agriculturists. It is difficult
to know if they were convinced by the arguments of the Whigs and Radicals that reform would cure their economic difficulties, but they
were willing listeners in their distressed state. Too, by giving
countenance to the reformers, the agriculturists of the kingdom could
demonstrate their disapprobation of the government's apparent inactivity in agricultural matters. Norfolk, a center of barley growing,
had a special grievance against the government. Barley growers, largely
dependent on sales to maltsters, held the malt tax in disfavor. When,
therefore, the government in 1819 raised the malt tax from 2s. 5d. per
bushel to 3s. 7 1/2 d. and retained the tax until 1822, Norfolk agriculturists felt themselves to be discriminated against.

Second, the Whigs themselves, by sponsoring and encouraging local
meetings as well as county meetings to petition against the government,
were unwittingly giving the agriculturist training in the methods of
extra-parliamentary agitation. As Professor Spring has observed, the
traditional advocacy by some Whigs of popular rights against the crown
led them, in the nineteenth century, to support actively a government
by public opinion--a move that was potentially anti-aristocratic.[41]
Norfolk Whigs had been especially active in the country campaign for
retrenchment and reform: the promotion by Coke and the local Whigs of
hundred meetings throughout the county ensured that an unusually large

number of Norfolk agriculturists were becoming familiar with and accostomed to the use of such meetings as legitimate organs for the expression of their grievances.

A third possible reason could explain Cobbett's success in Norfolk. It may be that Norfolk agriculturists were unusually self-assertive. Norfolk farming had long been famous, and its contribution to English agriculture was well known even abroad.[42] Much of the improvement in Norfolk agriculture had come about through the efforts of the larger improving farmers, for large farms were apparently an early feature of Norfolk.[43] Therefore, Norfolk farmers were usually quick to react when their economic interests were threatened.

A final reason for the rebelliousness of the Norfolk farmers in January, 1823, was the fact that they were tiring of the Whig slogans they heard at meetings--slogans which had diminishing relevance as the distress worsened. As "A Cultivator of the Soil" wrote to the Norfolk Chronicle shortly after the January, 1822, county meeting: "The threadbare topics of the American war, etc., etc., are quite sickening to us, when the emergency of our present distresses requires immediate attention. . . ."[44] Coke was especially prone to this kind of sloganeering, and liked to portray himself as a true and unaffected upholder of Whig liberalism against a tyrannical court.

In the weeks following Cobbett's Norfolk victory, the Whigs were forced into a defensive position at county meetings. The convening of numerous county meetings--in many cases by the Whigs--to influence the coming session of parliament now provided an ideal platform for Cobbett. He was not always successful,[45] but even when his "equitable adjustment" (as his program had come to be called) was not accepted in its entirety, some parts of his now famous Norfolk petition were often

incorporated into a meeting's resolutions. A Hampshire county meeting
in March, 1823, was attended by both Cobbett and Henry Hunt; Cobbett's
petition was voted down but the petition that was accepted carried a
resolution asking that the government consider the use of crown lands
and church property "for the benefit of the public at large"--an echo
of the most radical part of the Norfolk petition.[46] At a Somerset
county meeting in January, 1823, Sir Thomas Lethbridge, county M.P.,
shared the platform with Hunt; Lethbridge told the meeting that unless
the government acted to relieve the distress, he would continue to oppose it.[47] A Cambridgeshire county meeting in February, 1823, proved
to be a Radical forum. Samuel Welles, a Radical solicitor from
Huntingdon, attacked the Whigs as more averse to reform than the Tories.[48]
It appears that the Whigs boycotted the meeting to detract from its
respectability; the Cambridge Chronicle noted that although some 2000
attended "there was scarcely an individual of any consequence in the
county, who thought proper to attend."[49] However, the Whigs were out
in force at a Huntingdonshire county meeting in March, 1823.[50] Welles
again was present, denouncing the Whigs and advocating Cobbett's
Norfolk petition. He was answered by Lord Milton and Lord John Russell.
Lord Milton declared that the national debt should remain inviolate.
Lord John agreed: he pointed out that during the war when currency
was depreciated, public creditors received less than was their due.
"The creditor suffered then, and the debtor must suffer now." Lord
John then resorted to an unusual argument to refute Welles. Since
foreign relations were so uncertain (said Lord John) it was possible
that England might go to war soon, and therefore would likely have to
borrow. But if the national debt were tampered with, "how could we go

into the market for a loan, with such a stigma on our character?" In
his closing remarks, Lord John even seemed to defend the government,
for he reminded the meeting that the ministers had not done too badly
in the matter of retrenchment, having reduced taxes by £6 million in
two years.

Thus were the Radicalized farmers, led by Cobbett, forcing the
Whigs to retreat from their original program of retrenchment and reform. The Whigs were, however, soon released from this embarrassment.
Even as Cobbett enjoyed his greatest successes, the price of cereals
was beginning to rise. Wheat, which averaged 34s. a quarter in
November, 1822, exceeded 41s. in January, 1823, and 62s. 7d. by June.
This evidence of a return of prosperity to the countryside combined
with the influence of the Whigs (now used to dampen reform sentiment)
suspended agricultural interest in political activities. Much more
rapidly than it had arisen, the issue of reform sank from view. Indeed, for the next few years the subject virtually disappeared from
general public discussion. Farmers' attraction to reform had been
a curious and uncharacteristic episode: never again would reform have
much popularity with farmers. But the events of the 1820's showed
how far farmers were willing to go to force their attentions upon
parliament. Coached by the Whigs and encouraged by Cobbett, English
farmers--as in the case of Webb Hall's Agricultural Association--gave
indications of becoming a united political force. When agricultural
depression returned in the 1830's, farmers once again organized for
political action. There was an important change in their organiza-
tional efforts, however. In the 1830's farmers began to promote

75

protectionist candidates to parliament and to involve themselves directly in electoral politics. This is the subject of the following chapter.

Footnotes to Chapter III

[1] Indeed, as G.D.G. Cole noted in his biography of Cobbett, he was by nature an agrarian leader (G.D.H. Cole, The Life of William Cobbett (London, 1925), p. 256). But neither Cole nor other writers have given much information on Cobbett's rural activities. Even recent commentators tend to underestimate Cobbett's country campaign. For example, John W. Osborne, "William Cobbett and the Corn Laws," The Historian, Vol. XXIX, no. 2 (Feb. 1967), p. 195, writes that this phase of Cobbett's life is "anti-climactic."

[2] See Cole, Life of Cobbett, p. 279.

[3] William Cobbett, Rural Rides, Everyman ed. (1912), Vol. 1, p. 105.

[4] The Times, Jan. 7, 1822; Kentish Chr., Jan. 8, 1822.

[5] Cobbett, Rural Rides, Vol. I, pp. 105 ff.

[6] Ibid., p. 126.

[7] Worcester Jnl., Jan. 17, 1822.

[8] Bristol Obs., Jan. 28, 1822.

[9] Lord Brougham, The Life and Times of Henry Lord Brougham (New York, 1871), Vol. II, p. 261.

[10] Halévy, History, Vol. II, p. 104.

[11] Creevy Papers, ed. Sir H. Maxwell (New York, 1903), Vol. II, p. 37.

[12]Norfolk Chr., Feb. 8, 1822. Coke was certainly vigorous in his support of these meetings. He chaired two North Greenhoe hundred meetings, and attended other meetings of the hundreds of North Erpingham, Gallow, and Brothercross.

[13]Norfolk Chr., Apr. 6, 1822 and Apr. 20, 1822.

[14]Suffolk Chr., Feb. 17, 1821. The Taunton Courier of February 21, 1821, observed that at the dinner "was made the first explicit declaration by the Whigs on the subject of Parliamentary Reform; and before the cloth was drawn, a requisition for a county meeting on the subject, was signed by all the freeholders present."

[15]See Creevy Papers, Vol. II, p. 4.

[16]Oxford Jnl., Jan. 27, 1821.

[17]The Times, Jan. 19, 1821; and Kentish Chr., Jan. 19, 1821.

[18]Accounts of the meetings above may be found in The Times, Jan. 17, 1821, Mar. 21, 1821, Jan. 14, 1822, Jan. 31, 1822, Feb. 4, 1822, Feb. 5, 1822, and Feb. 19, 1822; Cambridge, Chr., Jan. 12, 1821; Suffolk Chr., Feb. 2, 1822.

[19]The Times, Jan. 13, 1821, Mar. 16, 1821, Apr. 22, 1822; Cambridge Chr., Apr. 5, 1822.

[20]The Alfred, Feb. 5, 1822.

[21]The Times, Jan. 14, 1822.

[22]Stamford Merc., Apr. 26, 1822.

[23] Sir Robert Heron, _Notes_ (Grantham, 1850), p. 134.

[24] _Norfolk Chr._, May 25, 1822, quoting from a Yorkshire journal.

[25] Richard Mackenzie Bacon, _A Memoir of the Life of Edward, Third Baron Suffield_ (Norwich, 1838), p. 159.

[26] Huskisson Papers, Add. MSS 38742, ff. 6-8.

[27] _Bristol Jnl._, Jan. 26, 1822.

[28] _The Times_, Apr. 22, 1822.

[29] _Kentish Chr._, June 7, 1822.

[30] _Norwich Cour._, June 15, 1822.

[31] _Bristol Obs._, June 19, 1822.

[32] This account of the meeting is taken from the _Norfolk Chronicle_, Jan. 4, 1823.

[33] A.M.W. Stirling, _Coke of Norfolk and his Friends_ (London, 1912), new ed., p. 483. Cobbett's victory was so startling that there were others who thought he must have been aided by government funds; it was necessary for Liverpool to declare it untrue. In a letter dated January 14, 1823, to the Duke of Buckingham, C.W. Wynn wrote: "Lord Liverpool positively asserts that he has neither directly nor indirectly pensioned Cobbett" (Duke of Buckingham and Chandos, _Memoirs_, vol. I, p. 410).

[34] Bacon, _Life of Suffield_, p. 173.

[35] *Works and Correspondence of Ricardo*, Vol. IX, p. 265.

[36] H. Twiss, *The Public and Private Life of Lord Eldon* (London, 1844), vol. II, p. 467.

[37] *The Times*, Jan. 8, 1823.

[38] *Worcester Jnl.*, Jan. 9, 1823.

[39] *Bury Post*, Jan. 8, 1823.

[40] Cobbett was so elated with his triumph that he established a newspaper, the *Norfolk Yeoman's Gazette*, to counteract the unfavorable press he had received, and to continue his propaganda among Norfolk farmers. It was short-lived, however (February-May, 1823).

[41] David Spring, *The English Landed Estate in the Nineteenth Century; Its Administration* (Baltimore, 1963), p. 21.

[42] For a comprehensive modern study of Norfolk farming, see N. Riches, *The Agricultural Revolution in Norfolk* (Chapel Hill, 1937). In France, Norfolk's agriculture was the best known and best described of any English county; see Andre J. Bourde, *The Influence of England on the French Agronomes, 1750-1789* (Cambridge, 1953).

[43] Riches, *Agricultural Revolution in Norfolk*, p. 65. See William Marshall's praise of the large, improving Norfolk farmers in his *Rural Economy of Norfolk* (London, 1787), Vol. I, pp. 37-8.

[44] *Norfolk Chr.*, Feb. 2, 1822.

[45]As at a Hereford county meeting in January, 1823 (Hereford Jnl.,
Jan. 23, 1823.

[46]Hampshire Telegraph, Mar. 3, 1823.

[47]Salopian Jnl., Jan. 29, 1823.

[48]Cambridge Chr., Feb. 21, 1823.

[49]Ibid.

[50]See the account in the Cambridge Chr., Mar. 14, 1823.

Chapter IV--The Farmer as Conservative: the 1830's

Farmers had few complaints about farm prices in the decade after
1822. Corn prices remained generally high. So high were they that
bread prices were forced up, adding to the misery of the distressed
working classes. The Tory government was therefore forced to modify
the protectionism of the Corn Law of 1815. In May, 1826, the government
introduced a bill which would allow bonded foreign corn in various
ports of the kingdom to enter the British market.[1] It also decided to
permit the entry of additional foreign corn, by order in council, if
it became necessary. Seen by most in parliament as temporary expedi-
ents, both measures passed.

In the following year the prime minister, Lord Liverpool, announced that the Corn Laws would again be altered. Within a few days
of the announcement, a fit of apoplexy put Liverpool on his deathbed.
In February, 1827, Canning became prime minister and thus responsible
for the Corn Law revision. Canning proposed a return to a sliding
scale of duties which had been in operation before 1815. The plan was
to impose a 20s. duty per quarter when domestic wheat prices were 60s.
a quarter. For every shilling that the price advanced above 60s the
duty would decrease by 2s.; hence when wheat rose to 61s., the duty
would be 18s., when it rose to 62s., the duty would be 16s., and so on.
Thus when the domestic price reached 70s. there would no longer be a
duty and wheat would enter free. The sliding scale would also work in
reverse: for every shilling's fall in price below 60s. there would be
an increase of 2s in duty per quarter.

Canning's death in August, 1827, and the succeeding short-lived ministry of Lord Goderich brought some confusion to the political scene and delayed any further action on the Corn Laws. With the formation of the Duke of Wellington's administration in January, 1828, however, the Corn Law was assured of another hearing by the appointment of Huskisson as Colonial Secretary. In March, 1828, the government introduced a corn bill modeled on the bill which Canning had proposed in the previous session. It retained the principle of the sliding scale with the difference that 66s. rather than 60s. would be the pivot point, and as the domestic price rose the duty would decline, not by 2s. intervals, but by a series of uneven jumps in the scale. When the domestic price reached 73s. a quarter only a nominal 1s. duty remained. For every shilling decline in the domestic price below 66s., the duty increased by 1s. The law also provided for other types of grain, each with their pivot points--barley at 33s., oats at 25s., and so on. The measure became law in June, 1828, and was to remain the basic Corn Law of England until its repeal in 1846.

The government's tampering with the Corn Laws had made the protectionists uneasy with the Tory party. Although agricultural protection remained the official policy of the Tories, ministers such as Liverpool, Robinson, Huskisson, and Canning seemed to be moving in the direction of freer trade policies. They were more in the Pittite tradition of firm fiscal management than Ricardians, but the effect was the same. Agricultural protection also remained the official policy of the Whigs. However, for the protectionists, there was a more worrisome trend in the Whig party: it had become increasingly committed to parliamentary reform. Farmers, after their brief

flirtation with reform in the 1820's, now saw that reform might be
inimical to the protectionist system. By enfranchising the industrial
northern cities, which were notorious for their free trade sentiment,
the Whigs could cause parliament to be flooded with free traders.
When the Whigs came to power in 1830 and introduced their Reform Bill,
farmers were thoroughly alarmed. As one land agent wrote to his em-
ployer: "the Tenants...are very apprehensive that in the event of the
Reform Bill passing, the House of Commons will be so constituted that
the duties on foreign Corn will be taken off, and free trade ensue...."[2]

The fear among farmers that urban interests would dominate rural
ones in the Whig reform scheme was not born out by the terms of the
Reform Bill of 1832. The Whig government--a government of aristo-
crats, after all--was not unsympathetic to the rural interest. The
Bill created new county seats as well as new urban ones. Whereas before 1832 each of England's counties had two M.P.s (with the excep-
tion of Yorkshire which had four) for a total of eighty-two, the final
version of the bill increased this number to 144. This was done by
creating seven three-member counties; separating twenty-six counties
into two divisions, each of which would return two members; increasing the Yorkshire representation from four to six; and allowing the
Isle of Wight a member. Put in another way, of the more than 140 new
seats created, sixty-two were given to English counties. Although it
might seem that the English counties would be underrepresented since
there would be 275,000 borough electors with 327 seats compared to
345,000 county electors with only 144 seats, in practice the balance
was redressed by the rural nature of many boroughs.[3]

Of equal importance to rural interests was a further extension of
the county electorate. On August 18, 1831, the ultra-Tory Marquis of
Chandos proposed an extension of the county electorate to include all
tenants at will who paid at least £50 annual rent. In introducing
his amendment to the Reform Bill, Chandos claimed the enfranchisement
of tenants as a matter of right. "If the landed interest was of any
value to the country, if any commiseration was due to the farmers for
their patient and loyal sufferings of late years, they ought not in
point of Representation to be worse treated than the householders in
towns..."[4] The amendment found immediate favor among the Tory gentry.
The Whigs, however, opposed the measure on the grounds that a tenant
at will (that is, without a lease) would be too subject to landlord
pressure at elections. But the House recognized that it would be unjust to give the vote to the 40s. freeholder, or to the £10 house-
holder and deny it to a tenant farmer who might be paying hundreds of
pounds in annual rent. Obviously, substantial farmers were as respectable a class of voter as those already enfranchised. Since the
proposal did extend the franchise, it suited the democratic views of
the Radicals and they offered their support. As a result, the amendment passed.

The general effect of the Reform Act of 1832, in short, was to
strengthen the farming electorate within the counties. In addition
to the £50 occupiers enfranchised by the Chandos Clause, the county
vote was also given to £10 copyholders and to long-term leaseholders
who paid at least £50 annual rent. Farmers could also qualify by
owning a 40s. freehold--an ancient right retained after 1832. Unfortunately it is impossible to determine the precise number of

farmers in each of these categories. A £50 occupier at will or a £50 long-term leaseholder, for example, could be a renter of a mill, an inn, or other commercial enterprise, and no farmer at all. In addition, there were counties with large industrial populations where the right of borough residents to vote in county elections gave a distinctly urban cast to the county electorate.[5] It seems safe to assume, however, that in most counties the three categories of occupier, leaseholder, and copyholder were comprised almost wholly of farmers, whereas only a minority of freeholders were farmers.[6]

Using these electoral categories (and bearing in mind the qualifications cited above), it is possible to make at least a rough calculation of the total number of farmers' votes in all counties. The most important category is that of occupier which in 1837 accounted for approximately twenty per cent of the total English county electorate. Some county divisions had very much higher numbers of occupiers. The highest were North Northumberland with 37.7%, the North Riding of Yorkshire with 34.6%, and Lincoln Kesteven with 34.0%. When farmers in the other categories—leaseholds, copyholds, and freeholds—are added to the occupiers, the farming electorate assumes impressive proportions.[7]

The year 1832 saw not only an enlarged farming electorate: it also saw the beginning of a renewed agricultural depression—the first since the early 1820's. Wheat fell from 60s. 4d. a quarter in August, 1832, to 52s. 6d. in December. A year later, it was 47s. 10d.; in December, 1834, it was 39s. 6d.; and by December, 1835, wheat stood at 35s. 4d. The low prices were probably due more to abundant harvests than to any other factor,[8] but farmers were convinced that previous imports and the threat of further imports had depressed prices. As prices fell, protectionism rose.

The effect of an agricultural depression upon an expanded farming electorate was, in a political sense, potentially significant. The first to recognize this were the Tories. The Tories were especially sensitive to events that might help them reconstruct their party after the election disasters of 1832. From the leadership downward--as Peel's Tamworth Manifesto indicated--Tories attempted to rethink their party in the light of the Reform Bill. Indeed, during the 1830's the Tories became better organized, more efficient, and perhaps more sensitive to public opinion than the Whigs. It should not be thought the Tories alone were responding to the beginning of a mass electorate, but it is the strength and quickness of their response by methods inherently uncongenial to them that is surprising. This resurgent Toryism was to a large degree spontaneous and manifested itself in the formation of local constituency conservative assocations as well as the agricultural associations with which this book is concerned.[9]

As protectionist sentiment rose in the countryside, the Tories realized that it was an issue which could be used against the Whigs. They hoped to convince farmers that they were, in spite of some regrettable lapses, more committed to protection than the Whigs. During the agricultural depression of the early 1830's, the Tories actively pursued farmers' votes. They did so neither in a coercive fashion nor relying necessarily upon traditional deferential support. Rather their method resembled a modern political campaign. Their approach

was twofold. First, they established numerous local associations designed to keep conservative candidates and conservative ideals before
the public eye. In the counties, the associations were often in the
form of agricultural associations, which would appeal specifically to
farmers. Second, the country Tories made it plain that their major
aim in standing for parliament was to promote agricultural protection.
In the 1830's there appeared a proliferation of protectionist "farmers'
friend" candidates at county elections. The Tory task was not an easy
one. There were other issues in the countryside which would neutralize
the protectionist campaign. Chief among these was religion. A dis-
senting farmer, for example, who felt his religion deeply might well
support reform and the Whigs in the hope of redressing grievances of
conscience. It would seem, however, that where economic and religious
interests clashed in the mind of a farmer, economics triumphed. This
worked to the Tories' advantage. Another advantage enjoyed by the
Tories was that although the Whigs had passed the Reform Bill (still
an object of suspicion among many farmers), they had accepted only
under duress the Chandos Clause enfranchising tenant farmers. A final
advantage to the Tories lay in the fact that the Whigs were in power
during the years of depression. The Tories could thus blame the Whigs
and receive a sympathetic hearing among farmers. As a result of
their country campaign, the Tories were more effective than the Whigs
in winning the farmers' support during the 1830's.

To illustrate the Tory country campaign of the 1830's and the
formation of the Tory-farmer alliance, three counties have been chosen.
They are Buckinghamshire, Essex, and Lincolnshire. In each, the
gentry (and in the case of Bucks, an ultra-Tory aristrocrat) were

active in appealing to the whole farming constituency--tenants and freeholders alike. In each, the constituency was somewhat different because of the variations in agriculture, but the campaign cry was essentially the same--protection to agriculture, especially the retention of the Corn Laws and the exclusion of all foreign agricultural produce.

In Buckinghamshire, the leader of the country campaign was Lord Chandos, the author of the Reform Bill amendment creating the enlarged county vote.[10] One would expect that Chandos could exert considerable influence during his campaign. As the eldest son of the Duke of Buckingham, he was the heir to the magnificent ducal mansion of Stowe and an estate of 67,000 acres. His family, the Grenvilles, was easily the dominant political force in Bucks with enough influence over several parliamentary seats to place them among the foremost political magnates in early nineteenth century England. Yet, behind the facade of immense power and influence exerted by the Grenvilles there was often electoral intransigence and occasionally even open rebellion.[11] Since the late eighteenth century, a growing electoral independence in the towns and villages of Bucks had forced the county leadership to exercise care in their relationship with their constituents. Influence alone was not enough to win electors' loyalty and their votes; and any attempt at autocratic control could result in an undesirable reaction at election time. Chandos sensed, in common with other local political leaders, the need to be responsive to a growing rural public opinion. His distinctive contribution was to extend this principle to a specific part of the electorate--the farmers.

Chandos' country campaign emphasized two issues--agricultural
protection and malt tax repeal, especially the latter. It is not en-
tirely clear why Chandos chose the malt tax as his major issue. Bucks
was not a particularly strong barley county: it was, in fact, becoming
known as a grazing and dairying region. Bucks farmers, however, were
strongly protectionist and they were probably willing to accept the
anti-malt tax quirk of Chandos in return for his general protectionist
support.[13] Farmers would certainly not question leadership from such
an exalted quarter. They were probably flattered by his attention,
for Chandos based his campaign on speeches to assembled Bucks farmers.
Chandos' theme at these meetings was unity in support of the farming
interest; as he put it in a meeting at Buckingham in 1832: "It is by
associating that we can best learn the general opinion; and it is by
union amongst ourselves that we can best carry the results of our de-
sires into execution."[13] Chandos hoped his example would influence
other landlords. At a farmers' dinner in Aylesbury in September, 1833,
he urged landlords to "mix a little more with their tenants and learn
their views and wishes."[14] Chandos apparently hoped to mold the farmers into an electoral force with himself as their head and in this,
as we shall see, he enjoyed some success.

To provide a local forum for the dissemination of conservative
views, Chandos became the force behind the Buckinghamshire Agricultural Association, founded in 1833.[15] Plowing matches and rewards to
industrious agricultural servants were combined on meeting days with
speeches against the malt tax or the advocacy of higher agricultural
protection. As the Bucks Association prospered, its membership increased. By its fourth anniversary meeting in 1837, some 1200 farmers

were enrolled.[16] A second association--the South Bucks Agricultural
Association--was founded for similar purposes in 1834. At one of its
meetings in September, 1836, Benjamin Disraeli, then a protégé of
Chandos, spoke of the growing political role of the Associations. It
was impossible, he said, to separate agriculture from politics. "Two
or three hundred persons could not be congregated together on any
subject of public discussion without having something to do with politics. The objects of the Agricultural Association were neither the
objects of party, nor were they factious; but they were political.
It was to no purpose to bestow rewards on ploughmen and peasants, if
the great principle of the Agricultural prosperity of the empire was
not kept in view. There existed a party in the state whose object
was the destruction of the Agricultural Interest. It, therefore, be-
hoved the country gentlemen and the farmers to have their eyes open
to their own interests and to assert them. The ploughs which that day
had been employed in the match would soon be rusty if the Association contented themselves with mere distribution of rewards to the
successful ploughmen."[17]

Using such politicized agricultural associations to the fullest
during the height of the anti-malt tax campaign in late 1834 and early
1835, Chandos exerted pressure upon the newly returned Tory government. At meetings in Buckingham, Aylesbury, and High Wycombe, Chandos
pledged his support to the farmers: "no power under Heaven," he
promised, "shall prevent me from coming forward and constantly claiming for you that relief which you so greatly need, and to which you
are so unquestionably entitled."[18] At the High Wycombe meeting in
January 1835, a Mr. Rolfe of Beaconsfield voiced the growing support

among Bucks farmers for Chandos: "Let the Yeomen and Farmers of this county set the example under the banners of Lord Chandos, and I am convinced that every county in England will respond to it...."[19]

How successful was Chandos' country campaign in bringing farmers within the ranks of the Conservative party? An answer must be predicated with some reference to the general political background in England.[20] The general election of 1832 had given the reformist Whig government a large majority: the Tories seemed decimated. But during the early 1830's, unanticipated difficulties took their toll of parliamentary support for the Whigs. Perhaps the greatest problem was Ireland. The appearance in the House of Commons in 1828 of Daniel O'Connell, one of the Irish leaders of Catholic Emancipation, signalled the modern beginning of the Irish independence movement. As a Catholic Irishman, he pressed hard in the Commons for a repeal of the Act of Union between England and Ireland. Some Whigs, such as Lord John Russell, favored a conciliatory policy to Ireland, but others, including Edward Stanley (later 13th Earl of Derby) leaned toward coercion. So divided were the Whigs on the Irish question that in May, 1834, four conservative Whigs (including Stanley) resigned from the government. Within a few months, the prime minister, Lord Grey, resigned over Irish matters, to be replaced by Lord Melbourne. Whig weakness persisted, however, and in November 1834, Peel and Wellington formed a Tory ministry--only three years after they seemed doomed to a long exile from power. Since it would be impossible for the Tories to face a parliament that was elected in 1832 and still inclined somewhat to the Whigs, a general election was called for January 1835.

The conduct of that election would determine the longevity of the
new Tory ministry, as Peel well knew. To ease the minds of a moderate
section of the electorate, he issued his famous Tamworth Manifesto.
In it he disclaimed any intention on the part of the Tories to tamper
with the Reform Bill which he regarded as a "final and irrevocable
settlement of a great constitutional question."[21] In the local constituencies, however, individual candidates sometimes took a less
moderate approach. Local Tory leaders knew that the conduct of great
questions of public policy such as the Irish question could influence
certain sections of the electorate to vote against the Whig candidates.
But they also knew that such questions would have less impact upon
the rural vote in the counties.[22] Consequently Tory candidates for
county seats and rural boroughs tended to stress agricultural matters
in their election appeal. The strategy was very nearly successful.
Although they did not quite manage to gain a majority over their Whig,
Radical, and O'Connellite opponents, they did gain 100 seats.[23] As
Greville observed of the election: "the county elections have given
a considerable turn to the state of affairs. The Conservatives have
been everywhere triumphant."[24]

The issues that divided the electorate during the county election
in Bucks were those between the supporters of dissent and the supporters of the agricultural interest.[25] Political work on Chandos'
part had assured the voters that agricultural protection was more important than religious controversy, and that the Conservatives were
sound on protection.[26] The result was a Conservative sweep--all
three of their county candidates were returned over two opponents. It
was nearly a complete reversal of the 1832 election when the county

had returned only one Conservative (Chandos). The <u>Bucks Herald</u> attributed the result to farming votes: "The Farmers rose to a man," it exulted.[27] One of the successful candidates, Sir William Young, claimed he had come forward "at the request of a large body of Farmers," backed by promises of support from the landed interest.[28] One of the defeated candidates, the Radical Dr. John Lee, declared after the election that the "real object of the Agro-Political dinners throughout this County has at length been clearly manifested, and too unfortunately accomplished."[29] Lee was very likely correct in his assessment. The farmers' dinners that Chandos promoted had paid off handsomely. At the chairing after the election, Chandos congratulated the county on the result and urged the tenants to continue exercising their new franchise. "The farmer of Buckinghamshire must now feel assured of the power that he holds in his hands. It is beyond description great. I told you it was within your grasp, and you have grasped it. (Protracted cheering.) The Fifty-pound Renter's Clause in the Reform Bill has been found efficient. It was obtained against the will of the ministry (Cries of 'By you, by you'), and you have shown that it was worthily bestowed—that it was not misintrusted to your care. (Cheers.) You see your power and you have exercised it; and I know it will not now be wrested from you, nor perverted by you."[30]

Thus far we have seen Chandos at work in local politics. Now we must examine his attempt to translate his local support into national policy at Westminister. Chandos was more than faithful in his parliamentary role as farmers' advocate. Time and again—almost doggedly—he sought agricultural relief from parliament. His first move in the reformed House of Commons was on April 26, 1833, when he

proposed a resolution on the subject of agricultural distress, calling
attention to the fact that there was no adequate relief for farmers
in the recent budget of the Chancellor of the Exchequer.[31] His motion,
however, failed. A few days later Chandos spoke in favor of the repeal of the malt duties, again without success.[32] On February 21,
1834, Chandos had a near success in the House of Commons as he moved
for the immediate reduction of agricultural taxes: he was defeated by
only four votes, 206 to 202.[33]

The following year, on March 12, he made a major speech in the
Commons on the Malt Tax setting out farmers' objections to it in the
most complete manner. Chandos insisted in his speech that the malt
tax not only injured the farmer by its harrassing method of collection,
but that it also tended to reduce consumption and hence the growth of
barley. To replace the revenue lost by malt tax repeal, Chandos suggested duties on raw spirits and foreign wines, articles which would,
if taxed, have the effect of "throwing on the higher classes more distinctly and fairly their share of the general burden."[34] The opposition of the government was decisive, however, and the motion to repeal
was lost by a large majority--350-192.

The surprising feature about Chandos' March speech was that he
made it in opposition to an ostensibly friendly government. The Conservatives under Peel had come to power by then, and were in office
until April, 1835. Chandos, in fact, had been offered a position in
the new government, but had refused when he discovered Peel's intention to retain the malt tax. The Conservative leadership was certainly unsympathetic to Chandos' campaign. Wellington had discouraged
Chandos, for he believed the revenue from the tax was necessary to

fiscal stability. Peel was opposed for the same reason. The leadership attempted to prevent Chandos from making his March speech. Prior
to the speech, a deputation of Conservative M.P.s--after attending a
meeting called by Peel--requested Chandos to desist.[35]   But he was
determined and delivered his speech as planned.

In spite of his defeats in the Commons and the opposition of some
of his followers, Chandos maintained a large minority for his motions.
This prompted him to move to the attack again in May, 1835. Noting
that wheat prices had declined from 110s. a quarter in 1800 to 38s. in
1835, Chandos declared "that the time had arrived when something must be
done by legislative interference to check this fall of prices to relieve
the farming population of some of their burdens...."[36]   Chandos also
sought to impress upon the House the high local rates that farmers had
to pay. "It was the land which was obliged to pay for the prosecution
of felons at Sessions and assizes; it was the land which was called upon to maintain and support prisoners; it was the land which had to de-
fray the expenses attending the building and repairing of bridges; and
it was the land which had to bear the cost of making and keeping in order the highways of the country."[37]   But again Chandos failed. Whig
spokesmen assured the House that it was conducting investigations into
the agricultural distress, and that Chandos' motion was premature. Chandos'
persistence was rewarded the following year when a parliamentary committee was appointed to inquire into the state of agriculture. The committee, however, came to nothing. An examination of the statements of the
witnesses reveals a wide variety of opinion as to the causes of the
continuing agricultural distress; and, perhaps as a result of the

failure of the committee members to agree, no recommendations were made.[38]

Chandos' agricultural activity in the mid-1830's proved to be the high point of his career. Apart from his continued association with the farmers, he cut a slight figure in parliamentary politics in the late 1830's. Although he was made Lord Privy Seal when Peel again came to power in 1841, a disagreement with Peel over the fiscally liberal budget of 1842 led to his resignation within a few months.[39] It was his last chance at high office. Even then financial disaster was closing round the Duke. By 1847 his debts reached £1,500,000, forcing the sale of Stowe the following year. Many of these debts had been incurred as political expenses. He had born most of the annual expense for voter registration while he was M.P. for the county. His lavish entertainment designed to cultivate country opinion had further drained his resources. At his death in a railway hotel in 1861, he was a poor man, reduced to writing his memoirs for money. He had, as The Times obituary noted of him, "lost everything but his name."[40] Nevertheless, he had contributed significantly to making the Conservative party the party of the farmers, not only in Bucks, but in other counties as well.

The country campaign in Essex assumed a slightly different shape than in Bucks. In Essex, there was no dominant aristocratic influence,[41] so that the gentry played the most important political role. Agriculturally, Essex was primarily an arable county with two-thirds of its area devoted to the growing of crops. Except in the Epping Dairying District and the grazing areas of the marshlands, most parishes had more than seventy per cent of their land in tillage.[42] Much of

this produce went to the growing London market. Essex farmers had
gained an enviable reputation as men of substance and active improvers.
By mid-century efficient drainage and widespread use of manures combined with good husbandry practices made Essex arable farming among
the best in the country.[43] It is not surprising that Essex farmers
should have been willing to participate in politics to preserve their
increasingly heavy capitalization in the land.

Prior to 1832 the county had usually divided its representation
between Whigs and Tories. The Whig influence in Essex was led by
C.C. Western of Felix Hall, MP for Essex since 1812. In the election
of 1832, however, Western, standing for the new county division of
North Essex, lost. This may be accounted for partially by Western's
ill health, and partially because of an inability to find a suitable
partner for Western in North Essex.[44] In addition, the Tories seem
to have been more assiduous in registering their known supporters.[45]
But the main reason for Western's defeat seems to have been the astute
Tory strategy of tarring Western with a free trade brush while por-
traying themselves as defenders of agricultural protection: this had
a predictable result in a farming community.

An important ally in disseminating the protectionist message was
the conservative newspaper, the Essex Standard. Months before the expected general election, the Standard published editorials, letters,
and addresses of every sort designed to make a common cause between
conservatism and protectionism and to associate the Whig candidates
with free trade. "The fact is," one editorial commented, "Mr. Western,
by supporting the present weak, inefficient, Free Trade Administration, through thick and thin...has rendered it dangerous...to the

Essex Farmers again to return him as their Representative."[46] Much
play was also made of the Whig administration's opposition to the
Chandos Clause. "The present Ministers have done nothing for the Farmers, and their having been allowed a vote was _forced upon the Whigs_ by
Lord Chandos," declared one letter to the editor.[47] Conservative
candidates in their election speeches continued the theme. Sir John
Tyrell castigated the Whigs for attempting "to annihilate the influence
of the Farmers and Yeomen of the country, by depriving them of all
share in the elective franchise....It was to the Tories that the agriculturist was indebted for that clause...which entitled him to a share
in choosing a representative...."[48] Tyrell's Conservative running
mate, Alexander Baring, spoke in the same vein.[49]

Tory strategy was successful as Baring and Tyrell triumphed over
Western and his youthful running mate, Thomas Brand, the nephew of
Lord Dacre. The final poll was: Tyrell--2448; Baring--2280; Western--
2244; Brand-1840. This was a dramatic reversal of the previous two
elections when Tyrell had lost in a three cornered fight.[50] The close
race between Baring and Western may well have been determined by the
support of the tenant farmers given to Baring. An examination of the
poll book for North Essex reveals that Baring and Tyrell carried a
majority of the fifty-pound occupiers in most of the electoral
hundreds.[51] As the _Essex Standard_ put it, Western had "so repeatedly
declared himself _to be a party man_ of the school of Lord Grey," that
farmers were compelled "to place their interests in other hands, be-
lieving that Mr. Western, in his zeal for his party, had abandoned
them...."[52]

To perpetuate the Conservative success in North Essex, the Hinckford Agricultural and Conservative Club was established in 1833. Hinckford Hundred was the largest of the Essex hundreds comprising forty-seven parishes and 170 square miles. A homogeneous lowland area located in the north central part of the county and long known for its cereal production, Hinckford was a natural selection for such a club.[53] The stated intentions of the Club were: to promote conservative candidates for the Northern Division of Essex; to encourage the circulation of newspapers and publications conducted "upon sound constitutional and Conservative principles;" and to guard the interests of agriculture.[54] On September 30, 1833, the Club held its first general meeting. Both the Conservative representatives for North Essex, Sir John Tyrell and Alexander Baring, were present and indicated their support for the Club. Baring praised its establishment because, he said, it "enabled agriculturists to obtain a superintendence and view of agriculture in general in the county, and to criticise the conduct of their Representatives in Parliament."[55] The history of the Club in later years makes it clear that it was an important forum for the dissemination of Conservative propaganda to local farmers.[56]

The Hinckford Club was only one of many established in Essex during the 1830's designed to protect agriculture. Following is a partial list: the Saffron Walden Agricultural Society, founded in 1833; the Winstree and Lexden Hundred Agricultural Association; Tendring Hundred Agricultural Association; Chelmsford and Essex Agricultural Association; Epping Agricultural Society—all founded in 1834; and the Colchester and adjoining hundreds' Agricultural Association (from 1839 styled the East Essex Agricultural Association), founded in 1835. The pages of the Essex Standard are filled with accounts of their meetings during the 1830's. These societies were not only local political forums; they also promoted agricultural improvement by sponsoring plowing matches, rewarding industrious laborers, and holding stock shows. But during times of acute depression, political concerns dominated agricultural ones.

Utilizing the methods described above, the Conservatives consolidated their hold on Essex during the 1830's. They won all four county seats in both divisions at the general election of 1835, and won all but one of the six borough seats. At the general election of 1837, this last Whig remnant, T.B. Lennard, was displaced by a Conservative at Maldon thus placing all ten Essex seats in Conservative hands. As Charles G. Round, one of the successful candidates for South Essex in 1837, put it: "while the £50 farmers have a vote, agricultural counties like Essex will return no reformers."[57]

The signs of a strong agricultural movement during the 1830's were also evident in Lincolnshire. It appears at first that upland wool and barley farmers were particularly active in seeking agricultural protection.[58] Upland wool growers had special grievances because of the imports of foreign and especially Irish wool in the late 1820's. Complaints such as those at the Lincolnshire Agricultural Society's meeting in 1829 that too little had been done for the wool grower during the recent parliamentary session were not uncommon.[59] Upland farmers were also very concerned about the malt tax since barley was mainly an upland crop. There were two county meetings in 1830 alone to protest the malt tax.[60] After 1832, however, sheep and barley prices remained relatively stable while wheat prices tended to

fluctuate considerably. This was to have a direct impact on Lincolnshire since wheat was beginning to replace barley as an important
arable crop. This was true even in the Wolds where wheat was making
its way under more intensive cultivation. Increased wheat acreage
in the Fens also contributed to a growing concern among Lincolnshire
farmers for a strengthened Corn Law.[61]

As in Essex a rash of new agricultural associations erupted in
Lincolnshire in the 1830's, coincident with the most acute phase of
the depression. The object of these associations was concisely stated
at the founding meeting of the Brigg Association in 1834: "to support
the interests of British Agriculture, by promoting union, disseminating
information, and affording facility to the collection and expressing
of the opinions of the Agriculturists to Parliament on matters affecting their interests...."[62] To promote this object, the following
Associations were established in Lincolnshire: the Boston; the Brigg;
the Horncastle; the Spilsby; the Great Grimsby; the Louth; the Gains-
borough; the Caistor; the Alford; the Barton; the Holbeach; the Long
Sutton; the Market Rasen. Even those associations originally established as agricultural improvement societies bent to the pressure
of the times. At the sixteenth anniversary of the Lincolnshire Agricultural Society in August, 1835, for example, the talk turned political after the stock show. The necessity of forming a more effective opposition to free trade theorists and Radicals was discussed;
one speaker strongly recommended "union amongst the farmers" as the
answer.[63] The Kesteven Agricultural Association, which had been
founded in 1826, was also turning to political questions by the early
1830's.[64]

Protection was, of course, not the only issue in Lincolnshire
politics. In a county which had an unusually high proportion of dis-
senters, religious issues--such as the church-rate controversy--could
also be important.[65] But it would seem that protection was a more
significant electoral issue. It is certainly true that the Conservative
protectionist platform bore electoral fruit in Lincolnshire as else-
where. The Northern Division of Lincolnshire (Lindsey) might be cited
as an example. Here, the initial difficulty for the Conservatives was
to overcome the influence of the great Whig landlord, Lord Yarborough
(created the Earl of Yarborough in 1837).[66] His influence was especially strong in the large upland farms around the family seat at Brocklesby
in the northeastern corner of Lincolnshire. A measure of Yarborough's
influence may be seen in the Lindsey election of 1832. Yarborough's
eldest son, C.A.W. Pelham, headed the poll in that year with 6554
votes; Sir William Ingilby--a Yarborough nominee-was second with 4748;
and the Conservative candidate, Sir Robert Sheffield, was last with
3858 votes.[67] Three years later, however, in the general election of
1835 the Whigs suffered a defeat when the Conservative T.C. Corbett
displaced Ingilby. In part the result can be explained by the character of Ingilby; he was eccentric in appearance and political style.
He had also become increasingly radical which seems to have alienated
some of his previous agricultural support. Nevertheless, the Conservatives, too, were severely handicapped in 1835. They seem to have
been poorly organized: there were two temporary candidates who started
(and resigned) before Corbett came forward only a few days before the
election.[68] And they had to work against the entrenched influence of
the Yarborough interest. In spite of these disadvantages Corbett

emerged the victor. The conservative <u>Lincolnshire Chronicle</u> claimed
that the farmers were chiefly responsible: "the principal farmers in
most parishes exerted themselves with an ardour worthy of the cause
they espoused," it wrote, "and to the exertions of the agriculturists,
and the agriculturists alone, is this glorious victory to be attributed."[69] The poll book for Lindsey verified farmers' importance to
the Conservative candidate: in fact, the farmers favored Corbett not
only over Ingilby, but over Pelham as well.[70]

During the next two years, however, Corbett failed to live up to
farmers' expectations. He did not, for example, support Chandos'
anti-malt tax campaign in the House of Commons. His unpopularity
forced his retirement at the election of 1837.[71] His place was taken
by R.A. Christopher whose seat at Well, near Alford, was in close
proximity to an important body of Lindsey electors—the farmers of
the coastal marshes. These smallholders were largely wheat farmers
and were among the most uncompromising protectionists in the farming
community.[72] The hope that Christopher could influence their votes
was probably the main reason for his selection as a Conservative
candidate. At the general election of 1837, Christopher and Pelham
(now Lord Worsley) were returned unopposed. Protection had once again
proved a potent issue in the countryside.

The evidence from these three counties goes far to explain the
decline of Whig electoral fortunes in the countryside during the 1830's.
The general election of 1832 had given the Whigs 102 of the 144 English county seats. At the general election of 1835 the Whigs gained
not a single English county seat and lost twenty-nine. The pattern
was repeated in 1837. By 1841, of the 144 English seats, the Whigs

held only twenty.[73] No doubt there are several reasons for the Whig

decline. Indecision and aristrocratic ennui were almost Whig tradi-

tions, as was faulty leadership. But Whig weakness was probably not

the major reason for Conservative successes at the polls. A Conserva-

tive party, recognizing the grievances of a newly important electoral

group and then capitalizing on them, must take much of the credit.

Footnotes to Chapter IV

[1]Information on Corn Law revision during the 1820's may be found in Barnes, History of the English Corn Laws, passim.

[2]The letter is from Martin Nockolds, agent of the Essex estates of Richard Benyon de Beauvoir, who resided in Berkshire (Berkshire R.O., Benyon Papers, D/EBy C19, July 11, 1831).

[3]For example, Aylesbury, Buckinghamshire, was in many ways more a small county than a borough. Enlarged in 1804, the borough was an extensive one, twenty miles long and twelve miles wide. As late as 1851 the population of 25,000 was overwhelmingly dependent on agriculture. Farmers represented the largest single occupational group and about one-third of the total electorate (for this information, I am grateful to Professor R. W. Davis in allowing me to see his manuscript, "Aylesbury Voters and Elections, 1847-1859," pp. 2-3). Similar "ruralization" of English boroughs was made possible by the Boundary Act, which accompanied the Reform Bill. It enlarged approximately 120 English boroughs, often by the addition of adjoining rural parishes (Norman Gash, Politics in the Age of Peel (London, 1953), pp. 67 ff. and Appendix B).

[4]Hansard, 3d ser., Vol. 6, Aug. 18, 1831, 273.

[5]The amended borough freeholder clause of the Reform Act of 1832 allowed borough residents to qualify as a county voter with respect to his borough property so long as that property was not used to qualify

the voter for a borough franchise. For a discussion of the importance of these voters, see E. P. Hennock, "The Sociological Premises of the First Reform Act: A Critical Note," *Victorian Studies*, Vol. XIV, no. 3 (March, 1971), pp. 321-27.

[6]Slightly less than thirty percent of the freeholders in North Lincolnshire (Lindsey) in the mid-1830's, for example, were farmers. This was calculated in the following manner. The total number of freeholders registered to vote for Lindsey in the 1837 election was 6564 as listed in Report on Electors Registered, and Voters Polled, at the last General Election, *Parliamentary Papers* (1838), IX. However, this source does not distinguish between farmer and non-farmer freeholders. The 1835 Poll Book for Lindsey does make this distinction, listing farmer freeholders at 1919, or 29.2% of the total freehold number of 6564. It should be pointed out that the number 1919 represents only those farmer-freeholders who actually voted; those who were qualified to vote but did not do so were not listed in the poll book. Hence, there is a conservative bias in the estimate of farmer-freeholders.

[7]See Appendix I.

[8]Barnes, *History of the English Corn Laws*, p. 223; E.L. Jones, *Seasons and Prices: the Role of the Weather in English Agricultural History* (London, 1964), pp. 165-6 .

[9]For a discussion of the constituency conservative associations, see Norman Gash, "Peel and the Party System," *Trans. Royal Hist. Soc.*, 5th ser., Vol. 1 (1951), pp. 47-69.

[10] I am indebted for the following discussion of Chandos to Davis, *Political Change and Continuity*, chs. 5 and 6; David Spring, "Lord Chandos and the Farmers, 1818-1846," *Huntington Library Quarterly*, vol. XXXIII, no. 3 (May 1970), pp. 257-81; David and Eileen Spring, "The Fall of the Grenvilles, 1844-1848," *Huntington Library Quarterly*, vol. XIX, no. 2 (Feb., 1956), pp. 165-190, and F.M.L. Thompson, "The End of a Great Estate," *Econ. Hist. Rev.* 2nd ser., vol. VIII, no. 1 (Aug., 1955), pp. 36-52.

[11] As Professor R.W. Davis has observed in his "Buckingham, 1832-1846: A Study of a "Pocket Borough," *Huntington Library Quarterly*, Vol. XXXIV, no. 2 (Feb., 1971), pp. 159-81.

[12] See the discussion of protectionism among Bucks farmers in Davis, *Political Change and Continuity*, p. 92.

[13] *Bucks Her.*, Oct. 13, 1832. The *Herald* was Chandos' mouthpiece.

[14] *Ibid.*, Sept. 28, 1833.

[15] The original mover in forming the association was Robert Sutton, a gentleman farmer of Cholesbury, Bucks (Davis, *Political Change and Continuity*, p. 118).

[16] *Ibid.*, May 6, 1837.

[17] *Ibid.*, Oct. 1, 1836.

[18] *Ibid.*, Nov. 1, 1834.

[19] _Ibid._, Jan. 31, 1835. Very likely the speaker was John Rolfe, who served as a witness during parliamentary hearings the following year. Rolfe, at that time, identified himself as a farmer and stock appraiser, renting between 200-300 acres (S. C. on Agriculture, _Parliamentary Papers_ (1836), VIII, pp. 76-95).

[20] The following account is based upon Asa Briggs, _The Age of Improvement_, (London, 1959), pp. 268 ff.

[21] Quoted by Halévy, _History_, vol. III, p. 178.

[22] As Professor Gash has observed in his _Politics in the Age of Peel_, p. 178.

[23] See the account of the election in Halévy, _History_, vol. III, pp. 179-82.

[24] Henry Reeve (ed.), _The Greville Memoirs: A Journal of the Reigns of King George IV and King William IV_ (New York, 1875), vol. II, Jan. 23, 1835, p. 340.

[25] Davis, _Political Change and Continuity_, pp. 120-21.

[26] The term "Conservative" is used hereafter to designate the main body of the Tory party. This is in accordance with contemporaries' change of terms in the early to mid-1830's (on this point, see Halévy, vol. III, p. 66-7n.3).

[27] _Bucks Her._, Jan. 17, 1835.

[28] _Ibid._

[29] Ibid., Jan. 24, 1835

[30] Ibid.

[31] Hansard, 3d. ser., vol. 17, Apr. 26, 1833, 679.

[32] Ibid., April 29, 1833, 729.

[33] Ibid., vol. 21, Feb. 21, 1834.

[34] Ibid., vol. 26, Mar. 10, 1835, 734.

[35] Norman Gash, Reaction and Reconstruction in English Politics, 1832-52 (Oxford, 1965), p. 142 and 142, n.2.

[36] Hansard, 3d. ser., vol. 28, May 25, 1835, p. 87.

[37] Ibid., 88-9.

[38] S. C. on Agriculture, Parliamentary Papers (1836), VIII, passim. For a discussion of the report, see Barnes, History of the English Corn Laws, pp. 227 ff.

[39] As Peel remarked of Buckingham's resignation: "The Duke of Buckingham remained to the last on cordial terms with us, ...and ultimately retired...because he was haunted by the recollection of pledges given at farmers' dinners, in the capacity he assumed of being especially the farmers' friend" (Charles Stuart Parker (ed.), Sir Robert Peel (London, 1899), vol. II, p. 520).

[40] The Times, July 31, 1861.

[41] Colin Shrimpton, "The Landed Society and the Farming Community of Essex in the late Eighteenth and Early Nineteenth Centuries," unpublished Ph.D. dissertation (Trinity Hall, Cambridge, 1965), p. 396.

[42] Elwyn A. Cox, "An Agricultural Geography of Essex, c. 1840," unpublished M.A. thesis (U. of London, 1963), esp. ch. 4 and 5.

[43] Ibid., p. 196.

[44] Essex R.O., Barret Lennard Corres., D/DL C60, letters from Western dated Aug. 16, 1832; Aug. 18, 1832; and Aug. 19, 1832; also D/DL C61 Courtauld to Lennard, Aug. 19, 1832; and D/DL C62, Rolph to Lennard, Aug., 1832.

[45] Essex R.O., Barrett Lennard Corres., D/DL C62, Knox to Lennard, Nov. 22, 1832.

[46] Essex Std., Sept. 29, 1832.

[47] Ibid., Dec. 22, 1832, "Address to the Electors, and especially the Farmers of North Essex," from H. John Conyers. See also Essex Std., June 16, 1832, letter from "An Elector of the Northern Division."

[48] Ibid., Sept. 22, 1832.

[49] Ibid., Aug. 18, 1832.

[50] Tyrell stood in 1830 also as a "farmers' friend" candidate; see Essex R.O., D/DL O 43/3, Essex County Election (Chelmsford, n.d.).

[51] See Appendix II.

[52] Essex Std., Dec. 29, 1832. The Conservatives also captured one of the two seats of the Southern Division of Essex. Hall Dare, who had made protection his major issue, was returned with the Whig, Sir T. B. Lennard. Later commentators attributed this result to the effect of the Chandos Clause (See Essex R. O., D/DL O 44/2, "The Election in 1847 in South Essex," which analyzes the 1832 election.).

[53] For a description of Hinckford Hundred, see Susan E. Cunningham, "Changes in the Pattern of Rural Settlement in Northern Essex between 1650 and 1850," unpublished M.A. thesis (Victoria University of Manchester 1968), chs. 1 and 2.

[54] See Essex R. O., D/DCm Z13 for broadsides published by the Club.

[55] Essex Std., Oct. 5, 1833.

[56] During the 1838 meeting, C. G. Round claimed that one "would be a bold man who would deny that the friends of the farmer are to be found among the Conservatives...." Nowadays, Round continued, "persons who are acquainted with the political world in its present aspect, are aware that Conservatism and protection to agriculture go hand in hand." (Essex Std., Oct. 12, 1838).

[57] Essex Std., Aug. 4, 1837.

[58] For Lincolnshire farming, see Joan Thirsk, English Peasant Farming: The Agrarian History of Lincolnshire from Tudor to Present Times (London, 1957), esp. ch. 10-13; and David Grigg, The Agricultural Revolution in South Lincolnshire (Cambridge, 1966).

[59] Stamford Merc. Sept. 4, 1829.

[60] Ibid., Jan. 15, 1830; Oct. 15, 1830.

[61] Olney, Lincolnshire Politics, pp. 106-7.

[62] Stamford Merc., Mar. 7, 1834.

[63] Lincolnshire Chr., Aug. 14, 1835.

[64] Ibid., Apr. 5, 1833; Mar. 13, 1835.

[65] Olney, Lincolnshire Politics, ch. 6.

[66] Ibid., pp. 94-100.

[67] Lincolnshire Chr., Jan. 30, 1835.

[68] See the accounts of the election in the Lincolnshire Chr., Jan. 16, 1835 and Jan. 23, 1835.

[69] Lincolnshire Chr., Jan. 23, 1835.

[70] The total votes for Corbett were 4321, of which 2384 were farmers. This includes farmers listed as freeholders, renters, copyholders, leaseholders, occupiers, and yeomen. Comparable figures for Pelham were 4479 total votes, of which 2201 were farmers. Votes for Ingilby totaled 4108, of which 1971 were farmers. The total votes are taken from p. 301 of The Poll Book for the Election of Two Members to Represent in Parliament the Lindsey Division of Lincolnshire (Stamford,n.d.). Farmers' votes were calculated by counting those listed as farmers in the poll book.

[71]Olney, <u>Lincolnshire Politics</u>, pp. 99-100.

[72]<u>Ibid.</u>, 30-1.

[73]Robert Blake, <u>The Conservative Party from Peel to Churchill</u> (New York, 1970), p. 46.

Chapter V--The Farmer as Conservative: the 1840's

Conservative warnings about the Whig intent toward the Corn Law
seemed confirmed in early 1839. Lord John Russell, Colonial Secretary
in the Whig government and leader of the House of Commons, announced in
January his resolve to seek a moderate fixed duty on corn as a substitute
for the sliding scale of the Corn Law. Although Lord John's proposal was
not specifically a free trade measure, a fixed duty could be set low
enough to effect a considerable reduction in protection. As one protectionist meeting put it, the fixed duty was "a mere catch" and only "a
first installment."[1] Protectionist farmers, therefore, continued to give
their support in the late 1830's and early 1840's to the Conservatives.
During these years, protectionists were up in arms in the countryside.
Farmers and gentry held numerous meetings to petition parliament against
any revision in the Corn Laws. The protectionists not only protested a
fixed duty, but they also complained about the recently established Anti-
Corn Law League. Farmers feared an alliance between the Whigs and the
Manchester free traders.

Meanwhile, Lord John urged on the cabinet his policy of a fixed duty
on corn. Politically speaking, Lord John's policy held a possible twofold benefit for the Whigs. The cry of Corn Law reduction and cheap bread
might strengthen the Whigs electorally in the great industrial towns.
Corn Law reduction could also, if combined with other tariff reductions,
encourage imports and bring in much needed revenue. By early 1841, Lord
John had won the cabinet to his policy, which was in time to include tariff
reduction as part of the forthcoming governmental budget. In parliamentary
divisions on the proposed tariff reductions, however, the Whig ministry

115

was defeated. On May 27, 1841, Peel moved for a no-confidence motion and
after a week of debate, he carried his motion by a single vote--312-311.
A dissolution of parliament followed.

The Whig electoral strategy of relaxed protective duties was now put
to the test. To some degree, as The Times observed, the cry of cheap bread
was successful.[2] At the close of the poll the Whigs maintained a majority
in the English and Welsh boroughs, albeit a slim one: 176 seats to 163.[3]
The Whigs also gained a majority of seats in Scotland and Ireland winning
thirty-one in Scotland to the Conservatives' twenty-two, and sixty-two in
Ireland to the Conservatives' forty-three. If English and Welsh county
seats are excluded, then the Whigs won 269 seats and the Conservatives 232
seats. But when the county seats are added the results are very different:
the Conservatives won 368 and the Whigs won 292. It is obvious that the
Conservatives won spectacularly in the counties; only 23 county seats went
to the Whigs while 136 went to the Conservatives. Representatives of
great Whig county families such as Lord Morpeth and Lord Milton in West
Yorkshire, Lord Howick in North Northumberland, Sir Charles Cavendish in
Sussex, failed at the polls.[4] As previously suggested, Whig weaknesses
and administrative malaise partially account for their defeat. Indeed the
contemporary estimate that "the sands of the Whig party were well nigh run
out" was not far wrong.[5] But, as in the two previous general elections,
credit must also be given to Conservative work in the constituencies: attention to organization and especially to the interests of the rural electorate had made its impact.

Three counties – Essex, Lincolnshire, and Cornwall – may serve as examples of the Conservative and protectionist campaign during the election

of 1841. In strongly conservative Essex, the outcome was a foregone conclusion. Even the Whig C. C. Western (now Lord Western) declared the Whig
adoption of a fixed duty as "fatally erroneous," and threw his support to
the Conservatives.[6] Protectionist speeches echoed throughout Essex, in
county and borough constituencies alike. In South Essex, T. W. Bramston
and George Palmer easily outdistanced R. Gardner Alston, their Whig opponent. In North Essex, C. G. Round and Sir John Tyrell were returned
unopposed. In the borough of Maldon the Conservative Quintin Dick promised
"to uphold the rights of the British Farmer," as did his colleague, John
Round.[7] At the close of the poll, Essex had once again returned ten Conservative representatives.

The Lincolnshire county elections showed a considerable gain for the
Conservative candidates. Prior to 1841 there were three Whigs and one Conservative representing Lincolnshire's two divisions: this ratio was re-
versed in 1841. In the Southern Division, represented by the Whigs Henry
Handley and G. J. Heathcote prior to 1841, Conservative strategy was designed to cast doubt on Whig fidelity to protection. Handley seems to have
been the special Conservative target, perhaps because of his more active
parliamentary role. As early as 1839 the Lincolnshire Chronicle directed
hostile fire toward him. When the election drew near remarks in the
Chronicle became more pointed. In an open letter to Handley from "A
Freeholder" in a June, 1841, issue of the Chronicle, Handley's "treachery
and ingratitude" was contrasted unfavorably with "the conduct of the Conservative party" which stood "pre-eminently forward as the protectors of
the Farmer...."[8] The loss of protectionist support was significant enough
to induce both Handley and Heathcote to retire before the election.

Heathcote's position had been further undermined when his father-in-law, Lord Willoughby, deserted the Whigs over protection. Heathcote stood for Rutland, succeeding his father at the election. Thus were two protectionist Conservatives, Christopher Turnor and Sir John Trollope, returned for South Lincolnshire.[9]

Generally speaking, Whigs from agricultural districts were placed in an awkward position in the election of 1841. Constituency pressure to give protectionist pledges, if acceded to, would clearly place Whig candidates at variance with official Whig policy. Lord Worsley's position in North Lincolnshire illustrated this dilemma. He felt it necessary to assure his constituents that he remained a firm protectionist; in an open letter to Lindsey electors he pledged "every opposition" to the Whig-endorsed fixed duty.[10] Yet during the parliamentary debate on Peel's no-confidence motion in May he supported the continuance of the Whig government. His argument was that it would be wrong to turn out a government on the basis of only one of its policies--in this case tariff reduction. Rather, he said, a government ought to be judged on the whole of its merits. Although on the question of the Corn Law, "he felt he had only one course to pursue," - to vote against the Whigs, - he could not support the no-confidence motion.[11] His Conservative colleague from Lindsey, R. A. Christopher, denounced Worsley's continued support for a ministry that had promised to alter the Corn Laws: it was "an insult," he declared, to the agricultural constituency that he represented.[12] Nevertheless, Worsley was returned with significant farmer support as the only Whig county MP for Lincolnshire. Worsley's protectionist pledge and the high personal regard for him in the county (which even the Lincolnshire Chronicle admitted) carried him to victory with Christopher.[13]

Protection as a successful electoral slogan for the Conservatives in
1841 was not limited to the best farming regions in England. Cornwall pro-
vides an example. Its agriculture, unlike the more advanced farming regions
of Essex and Lincolnshire, had long been considered backward. At the close
of the eighteenth century the agricultural writer William Marshall had
damned Cornish agriculture with the faintest praise when he wrote after
a visit there that he was "agreeably disappointed" with it--by which he
meant that the county was not as wretched as he had expected it to be.[14]
Although there were some improvements in the first decades of the nineteenth century, obsolete practices persisted. A further difference between
Cornwall and other counties lay in the fact that Cornwall had a greater
number of small farms than any other county.[15] There was only one great
landowner in Cornwall--the Duchy. In addition to the Duchy were other, less
large, estates owned by Lords Falmouth, Godolphin, and the Grenvilles.
These landlords, like the Duchy, were absentee. Other absentee estates were
owned by the banking family of the Barings, the Dukes of Bedford, and nabobs
like the Barwells.[16] Perhaps the lack of active resident landlords in a
county of smaller, poorer farms partially explained the limited advance of
Cornish agriculture.

A poor state of agriculture did not prevent an active farmer's movement. In the beginning of the 1830's, it seems to have been largely Whiggish in sentiment. This may have been due to the influence of the tithe
question, an especially lively issue in nonconformist Cornwall. Under the
leadership of a noted farmer and agricultural improver, John Penhallow
Peters, the tithe question, reform, and Whiggism became inextricably mixed
in Cornwall.[17] By driving home the argument that a reformed parliament

would be more responsive to farmers' grievances over tithes, Cornish Whigs could pose themselves more easily as the farmers' friends than could the long-governing Conservatives. At the election of 1832 the Conservatives countered with a characteristic protectionist campaign[18] but were unsuccessful, since all four county members returned were Whig reformers.

In the long run, however, their association with protection benefitted the Conservatives. When it became clear that the commutation of tithes in 1836 was not improving the economic position of the farmer, dissatisfaction grew among previously Whiggish farmers. At the general election of 1837 the Conservative Lord Eliot was returned head of the poll in East Cornwall, the more agricultural of the two divisions. His campaign seems to have been directed mainly toward the farmers, although his protectionist advocacy included protection for the mining interests as well.[19] A Whig, Sir Richard Hussey Vivian, was returned with Lord Eliot for the division. At the 1841 general election, Lord Eliot was assured of return, but Sir Richard was forced to retire because of his free trade views.[20] The contest for Sir Richard's vacant seat was fought between J. S. Trelawny and William Rashleigh of Menabilly. Trelawny's advocacy of a fixed duty on corn placed him squarely in the Whig camp and was too mild a protectionism for Cornish farmers. Rashleigh presented himself as a "farmers' friend" candidate, and by appealing directly to farmers, emerged the victor (due in some part, no doubt, to his father's influence).[21]

As Essex, Lincolnshire, and Cornwall illustrate, protectionist farmers and gentry turned out in force to assure Peel's victory in 1841. In the words of the Bucks Herald, the 1841 election had "vindicated the Farmers' rights, by returning to Parliament, a more decided majority to support the Corn Laws" than ever before.[22] Farmers believed that the Conservatives would preserve the Corn Laws intact. Had not Peel in his own election address to his constituents at Tamworth upheld the principles of protection?[23]

Yet within less than a year the Corn Laws, untouched since 1828, untouched indeed in more than a decade of Whig administrations, were significantly altered. Sir Robert Peel himself was the architect of Corn Law revision. In both the Corn Law revision and his later general tariff reduction schemes Peel's aim was twofold - to reduce government deficits and to reduce the high price of consumer goods. By reducing duties far enough below the prohibitive level Peel hoped (as had Lord John before him) to encourage the growth of imports, thus replenishing the treasury with import duties. By reducing the high prices of consumer imports Peel also hoped to placate an agitated country. England by the early 1840's had experienced several years of severe industrial depression. Outbreaks of public disorder by the resentful unemployed had already occurred. Unless something were done, more serious outbreaks were likely. "We must make this country a cheap country for living," Peel wrote to Croker in 1842.[24] "The danger is not low price from the tariff, but low price from the inability to consume--from the poor man giving up his pint of beer, and the man in middling station giving up his joint of meat."[25]

In advocating a revised Corn Law, Peel felt no inconsistency with his previous statements on agricultural protection. As prime minister, his viewpoint had to be wider than that of any one class--certainly wider than that of the farmers and gentry whose more limited vision rarely extended beyond their own corn fields and cattle yards. Peel maintained that he was still protecting agriculture, but that there could never be an absolute protection. Only a fair protection could work.[26] The theme of a fair

protection Peel carried into the House of Commons when he introduced the
principles of a new corn bill on February 9, 1842. "The protection which
I propose to retain," he told the Commons, "I do not retain for the espe-
cial protection of any particular class. Protection cannot be vindicated
on that principle."[27] The proposed measure was not designed to appeal to
the two extremes of unlimited protectionism and complete free trade but
to "that intermediate class of persons" who would consider the new law
"just and reasonable."[28]

The proposed measure was clearly less protectionist than the law of
1828 which it replaced. The law of 1828 had imposed a duty of 20s 8d a
quarter on imported wheat when the domestic price was 66s a quarter. The
new measure imposed a 20s duty at the much lower level of 51s and de-
creased the duty as the domestic price rose. This meant that when domestic wheat prices reached the old pivot point of 66s (which had called for
a 20s 8d duty), the duty was to be only 7s. As in the old law, there was
a nominal 1s. duty after the domestic price exceeded 73s. a quarter.[29]

Given the tone of county meetings during the campaign of 1841, when
agricultural members pledged themselves to uphold protection, one would
have expected county members to have been vocal in opposition to the proposed new corn bill. But they were strangely silent. R. A. Christopher
did propose an amendment which would have increased the duty at the lower
end of the price scale by 5s. a quarter, but withdrew it before it came to
a vote.[30] One Conservative county member, Sir Edward Knatchbull of East
Kent, even defended the proposed bill as giving "general satisfaction" to
the agricultural interest.[31] Only Lord Worsley consistently opposed Peel's
corn bill as insufficiently protectionist. On April 7, the final day of

debate, the free trader C. P. Villiers taunted the county members for
silently acquiescing in the new Corn Law. The county members seemed a
"peculiarly docile party," Villiers declared; indeed, "they seemed disposed to go wherever the right hon. Baronet [Peel] would lead them...."[32]
Responding to Villiers, Sir John Tyrell of Essex declared that members
representing the agricultural interest had been falsely accused "of sacrificing the interests of the agriculturists at the shrine of political
principle."[33] Not so, said Sir John; his constituents approved of his
action. Those "who threatened the county members with being called to an
account at the hustings for having sacrificed the interest of the agriculturists in supporting the Corn-bill" were mistaken.[34] H. G. Ward of Sheffield was unconvinced. He prophesied that agricultural members "would find
it a difficult matter to reconcile their professions to their constituents
with their conduct in that House."[35]

Ward was correct in his prediction; agricultural members returning to
their constituencies discovered an alarmed electorate. Lincolnshire was
one of the most active counties against the measure. As one report had it:
"All Lincolnshire is in a flame."[36] Even R. A. Christopher, who had done
more than most county members to uphold protectionism, was not immune from
criticism. At a Lincolnshire county meeting in early April, he attempted
to defend himself by suggesting that an overly vigorous opposition to the
corn bill might have endangered the Conservative government. But to Mr.
F. Iles this was "no excuse;" he suggested that the meeting make clear to
Christopher "he had not done his duty, and that the agricultural members
had not done their duty."[37] An Essex county meeting had even more severe
reprimands for its representatives.[38] John Bawtree flatly declared himself

dissatisfied with the Essex county members. "They were looked up to as the protectors and defenders of agriculture; and whenever they have appeared before their constituents on the hustings, I would ask whether "protection to agriculture" was not their watchword? (Cheers.) Were their banners not emblazoned with the words "The Farmers' Friend"" Yet, he continued, their representatives had offered no parliamentary opposition to the Corn bill. "I do consider that it was in the power of those gentlemen to have made such a stand on the duty to be imposed... as would have compelled Sir Robert Peel to leave his high station, and enter into a compromise. (Hear, hear.) If twenty county members had stepped forward, fifty others would soon have followed them, and he must at last have given way." Sir John Tyrell--to whom the meeting must have been a shock, if his earlier parliamentary pronouncement is to be believed--asked for an understanding of county members' position. At Westminster, he said, there were "no separate pigeon holes for gentlemen with crotchets on the Corn-law, but you must say aye or no." T. W. Bramston (M. P. for Essex, South) attempted to defend himself by blaming the farmers for not stepping forward earlier with their opinions on the Corn Law. "During the whole time that measure was before the Commons not a representation from an individual, or from any body of individuals, did I receive on the subject." This was met with a shout from the crowd: "You ought to have known your duty." Mr. Algernon White queried Bramston further on his statement. Was it necessary for Bramston to be reminded of his constituents' wishes "elected as he was but a twelvemonth ago in this place?"

Essex and Lincolnshire protectionists were not alone in expressing their dissatisfaction with their parliamentary representatives. Agricultural meetings

in other counties were as harshly critical. At the Royal Bucks Agricultural Association meeting in February 1842, Capt. Hamilton, MP for Aylesbury,
met the complaints against his conduct with a long and apologetic speech.
"If any man living could have pointed out to him a clearer road to take,"
he said, "he... would cheerfully have pursued that course. He had attended
the meeting held at Sir R. Peel's the day before the scheme was submitted
to Parliament, and he confessed he had expected that some gentlemen connected with an agricultural county would have expressed his dissent on the
subject. No such thing had, however, happened. There had been no instructions sent from constituent bodies, and hence the representatives of the
agriculturists were left in the predicament either to adopt Sir R. Peel's
plan, or to throw the whole question into a state of indescribable confusion...."[39] Cornwall, too, expressed its opposition to the Corn Law alteration. At a meeting of the Hundred of East held at Callington in April
1842, Deeble Boger voiced the common sentiment when he declared that the new
Corn Law "had created a degree of anxiety in the breast of those practical-
ly affected by it...."[40]

It is clear that the Conservative leadership had placed agricultural
members in an embarrassing position. Torn between the wishes of their
constituents and the exigencies of high policy as outlined by Peel, they
appeared confused before their constituents and cowed in the House of Commons. Members had promised their constituents to follow one course of
action only to adopt another in parliament. But political trimming could
be carried only so far. Pushed by an aroused agricultural interest, members were more alert when the next challenge to protection appeared. It
soon came in the form of Peel's tariff revision scheme introduced in the

House on May 10, 1842. This was part of Peel's general plan for reducing the price of consumer goods. It proposed reductions on hundreds of dutiable articles, including those on agricultural products. From the protectionist point of view, the most significant addition to the list of tariff reductions was farming stock. Stock, previously prohibited, was now to be admitted with only nominal duties: for example, the duty on live oxen, bulls, and horses was to be one pound per head; cows 15s. each; and sheep 3s. each.[41] Stock farmers, who had a vested interest in cheap grain, and had hitherto been more inclined to free trade than arable farmers, found themselves threatened by live animal imports. The effect of the tariff revision, then, was to consolidate further the protectionist strength among farmers.

As the debate on the new tariff measure lengthened over the next two weeks, a revolt among the Conservative agricultural members emerged. On May 23 it came to a head. That day, William Miles, member for East Somerset, introduced an amendment to the proposed tariff reduction that would impose duty on live animals by weight rather than by head. If that principle were granted, the agriculturists then hoped to impose a duty per pound that would greatly exceed the duty per head. Miles, in introducing his amendment, made it clear he objected to any further reduction of agricultural protection: "he and his friends had gone along with the right hon. Baronet as far as they could; they had not opposed the Corn-bill; they had agreed to it in silence... But the time of silence was now passed; it was their duty to their constituents to defer no longer stating their sentiments on this part of the measures of the right hon. Baronet."[42] It was an ineffective revolt, however, and easily crushed. The amendment lost by 380 votes to 113, with the Whigs and Radicals supporting Peel.

To protectionist farmers, the first session of Peel's government was disastrous. As Sir Henry Smyth, MP for Colchester, admitted to a meeting of the Hinckford Agricultural and Conservative Club: "The motto of "The Farmers' Friends" on our banners has been thrown in our teeth, and we have been told that Sir Robert Peel and the present Government have not fulfilled your expectations or carried out the Conservative principles on which they were called to administer the affairs of the county."[43] One suspects a fair amount of plain speaking between the protectionist electorate and their representatives during the parliamentary recess. Agricultural members could no longer disregard protectionist demands and expect to remain on equable terms with their constituents. But the feeling in the countryside was that the worst was over. The new Corn bill and tariff reduction scheme were comprehensive measures: they would need time to work. Agricultural matters seemed settled.

No sooner had the following parliamentary session opened, however, than there were intimations of a further change in the recently passed Corn Law. On February 16, 1843, the Colonial Secretary, Lord Stanley, told the House that negotiations with Canada were preparing the way for a further reduction of the duty imposed on Canadian wheat imports.[44] The Corn Law of 1842 had enacted a schedule of colonial preferences that allowed corn from British possessions to enter at a much lower duty than foreign wheat. For example, when the British domestic wheat price was less than 55s. a quarter, the duty on colonial wheat imports was only 5s. (compared to 18s. to 20s. under the foreign wheat schedule); above 58s. the duty was only 1s. The Peel ministry now proposed to reduce the duty on Canadian wheat to only 1s.

with a comparable duty on Canadian flour.[45]

At this news there was uproar in the countryside. Farmers felt that the easier passage of Canadian wheat was simply one more step on the road to free trade. They feared, too, that the government could not prevent the smuggling of American wheat into Canada: they had visions of illegal American wheat combining with Canadian to flood the English market. English farmers would then face the competition of an entire continent's productive capacity. However irrational these fears may appear, they were real enough to the farmers. Although county meetings protesting the Canadian Corn Bill are too numerous to cite in full, a few examples may illustrate the intensity of feeling among the protectionists. When, at a meeting of the East Essex Agricultural Association, C. G. Round (member for North Essex), urged that petitions against the measure be delayed, Mr. T. Baker of Lexden vehemently objected: "I am sorry, as a humble individual, to differ from the gentleman [Round] who has just sat down; but after twelve months' experience of the attacks made upon the agricultural interest I must doubt as to the motives of those who bring forward this measure." He reminded the meeting, too, that their MP's had been less than active in supporting farmers' interests. He concluded: "I trust that my brother farmers, who have already found themselves deceived by professions, will no longer be so: I trust that they will in future support men of principle—men who will uphold their interests. I hate party; and I confess I do not know what the word "Conservative" means....We must put by party—we must come forward and support our interests."[46] A Mr. Sheppard echoed similar sentiments at the Chelmsford Farmers' Club meeting that same week: "We begin to feel that our representatives should make a stand; they are too liberal in the House to the manufacturers; we want to legislate for ourselves and not for the benefit of foreign nations."[47]

In Leicestershire, too, there was anger at the actions of the Peel government. At the Waltham Agricultural Society's meeting, a Mr. Bradford of Stonesby, who identified himself as a tenant farmer and a Conservative proclaimed himself a disappointed man "for the Conservative Government had not carried out those measures which the farmers expected...." He charged Peel with committing a "gross breach of faith" with the farmers. "They had a right to expect some little protection from this Government...."[48] In Lincolnshire, at a meeting sponsored by the Stamford Agricultural Society to protect the Canadian Corn Bill, a Mr. Fountain of Deeping urged the county members (of whom Sir John Trollope was present) to oppose in parliament any further alteration in the Corn Law "thereby showing to the government that if they wished to remain friendly with the farmers, they must cease the continued nibbling at their interests."[49]

Farmers' pressure had an impact. In an unusual move MPs began to pledge themselves at these county meetings specifically to oppose the Canadian Corn Bill. At the Bourn (Lincolnshire) Agricultural Society, Sir John Trollope stated his opposition to the proposed bill.[50] At a Grantham meeting Christopher Turnor pledged the same.[51] At a Wallingford (Berks.) Agricultural meeting, W. Blackstone, MP for Wallingford, promised "to take up an independent line in Parliament, and would oppose with all his power any measures which might tend to decrease that amount of Protection which he considered necessary for the Farmers...."[52] How many more pledges were given is unknown, but it is clear that farmers were actively seeking them. More than at any time since the agricultural depression of the early 1820's,

farmers were taking the initiative. As a letter from "A Lincolnshire Farmer" put it to "The Farmers of England:" "...the stream of our fortunes is
careering away in an impetuous torrent towards the open gulf of Free Trade;
we must stem it quickly, and with energy, or we are lost! We must stem it
by our unaided efforts, as we have been deserted by our natural leaders..."[53]

As a result of the pressure generated by the county meetings, Stanley's
formal introduction of the Canadian Wheat Bill in the House of Commons on
May 19, 1843, was marked by a curious defensiveness. He claimed that "gross
misrepresentations" had been made with reference to the government's intention.[54] The bill was not brought forward as a measure for the promotion of
free trade, Stanley stated, but rather "as a great boon to one of our most
important colonies. I submit it to the House as a colonial and not as a
fiscal question....It is a measure apart from the Corn Law—apart from any
question of free trade."[55] The intention was to promote Canadian agriculture and to strengthen the colonial system.[56] Stanley's defense of the
proposed bill did not convince the agricultural members.

On May 26, Lord Worsley offered an amendment which would have killed the
bill. Support for Worsley came from the agricultural members who again
cited farmers' opposition. The government had sufficient votes, however, to
defeat the amendment. Within a week Worsley proposed another amendment,
calling for postponement of the second reading. Once again the government
beat back the attempt. On June 15 a final attempt to stop the bill was made
when Col. Sibthorp, member for Lincoln, moved to postpone. Government
victory over Sibthorp's motion removed the final impediment in the House of
Commons and the bill received the royal assent on July 12.

By the end of 1843 the farmers of England were angry and disillusioned with the Conservative government. There were numerous reports that the farmers were abandoning the Conservatives. Lord Redesdale was worried enough to inform the Governor-General of India about the matter. Low Agricultural prices he wrote, and the uncertainty of maintaining the Corn Law had "weakened our hold over the farmers...."[57] The Governor-General, Lord Ellenborough, had already received a report from Lord Colchester that the 1842 tariff jeopardized the seats of those agricultural members who had supported it.[58] There was even gleeful talk among the Whigs that they would soon be in office.[59]

Farmers' frustration was exacerbated by their growing fear of the Anti-Corn Law League. From the beginning of 1843, the League, in a belated recognition of the importance of the rural electorate, had turned its efforts to the countryside.[60] The League sent its agents into agricultural areas to conduct mass meetings and distribute propaganda. By September, 1843, a packet of League tracts had been distributed to each elector in twenty-four county divisions and 187 boroughs.[61] Cobden himself began to appear at League rallies in the countryside. By July he was at Colchester, Essex, in the heart of the protectionist country.[62]

The League believed that farmers were free traders at heart. They also believed that farmers only needed encouragement to speak out against a protectionist aristocracy: this was the aim of their country campaign. How mistaken they were is evident from the response of the farmers in forming an anti-League organization, the most significant milestone in the farmers' political coming of age. The Anti-League had its origins in a suggestion made by the Rev. J. Cox at a November, 1843, meeting of the Hinckford

Agricultural and Conservative Club.[63] The Rev. Cox proposed that the various
agricultural improvement societies in the county be remodeled into protectionist societies. The suggestion caused a flurry of interest as expressed
in a series of letters to the _Essex Standard_. A letter from Robert Baker of
Writtle (near Chelmsford) stated the case for an Anti-League perhaps best of
all. Baker, a land-valuer and tenant farmer who had long been active in the
Chelmsford and Essex Agricultural Society, was a man of some local standing.[64]
He denounced the "fallacies and false statements" of the League, and urged
"all the power of the agricultural body into opposition..."[65] The following
week Baker chaired a meeting of farmers at Chelmsford to discuss methods of
countering the League's propaganda in rural districts. Two weeks later, on
December 22, 1843, the first meeting of the newly formed Essex Agricultural
Protection Society was held with Baker serving as chairman. To the nearly
1000 men assembled at the Saracen's Head Inn at Chelmsford, Baker made it
clear that the new society was organized by farmers to promote farmers'
interests: "I stand here as a humble individual, and as a tenant farmer,
and beg to state in that character I have addressed several letters to you,
because I have always felt that the interest of the tenant occupier is very
much at stake in the question--and indeed more so than the interest of any
other class of the community.... This meeting has been called to show that
the tenants can come forward and combine in their own defence...to resist
attacks upon them...." That Baker was thinking of a movement in broader
terms than a single county is clear from his concluding remarks: "I have
no doubt this will be followed out by the tenantry of England generally, and
that such a flame will be lighted up in Essex as will extend to the other
counties, and show to the League that they have raised a body more powerful

and formidable than themselves."[66]

News of the Essex Association spread rapidly. Within a month, meetings were held in Lincolnshire, Northamptonshire, Derbyshire, Kent, Oxfordshire, and in Peel's own constituency of Tamworth.[67] The rapid growth of the farmers' meetings soon occasioned comment from the metropolitan press. The Morning Post--soon to be a firm supporter of the farmers' organization-- gave only grudging adherence to the movement at first because of its genesis among farmers: "We cannot but lament that the impulse to honourable action should have to come from below, and that it should be necessary for the farmers to force a sense of political duty upon country gentlemen, instead of country gentlemen being foremost in the political field to defend the cause of the farmers: but in default of what is best, we must welcome what is next best, and we rejoice that the farmers are now so energetically re- minding their political representatives of what ought to be done."[68] The Spectator, too, was impressed by the evidence of farmers' initiative: "Without any allusion to 'ill weeds,' we must confess that the agriculturist movement grows apace: it is becoming quite 'formidable.' The English agri- cultural countries are all alive with Protectionists marshalling themselves in the new organization.... The tenant-farmers assemble in hundreds; sub- scriptions begin to be worth mentioning...."[69] Even The Times, which thought the demands of the League too extreme, wrote in encouraging terms of the new farmers' organization.[70]

A burgeoning farmers' movement of national proportions could not leave aristocratic interests untouched. Inspired by the farmers' organization (and perhaps motivated to control it) an aristocratic protectionist society was formed in February, 1844. Their first meeting was held at the Duke of

Richmond's London House in Portland Place.[71]   A day or two following that
meeting, a farmers' meeting, chaired by Robert Baker, was held at the Free-
mason's Tavern in London. The farmers, too, had decided to establish a
central office in order to coordinate the local farmers' protectionist
societies. There were 250 present from nine counties; also present were
George Darby, MP for East Sussex and William Miles MP for East Somerset,
emissaries from the recently formed Portland Place group.[72] During the
course of the discussion it was decided to combine the two societies. A
provisional committee of twenty-two delegates was then sent to Portland
Place. At the Duke of Richmond's house--where were present Richmond, the
Duke of Buckingham (as Chandos now was), the Duke of Leeds, and forty or
fifty other landlords--a discussion ensued as to the shape that the new
society should take. During the discussion, Richmond reportedly supported
the idea that the farmers should have "a very full representation" in the
management of the society's affairs.[73] This was to be furthered by the
constitutional structure of the society which consisted of a president,
vice-president, four trustees, and a managing committee of forty members,
twenty of which should always be tenant farmers. After Richmond and Buckingham accepted the two major offices and the other officers had been selected, "the deputation of tenant-farmers withdrew, much gratified with
the proceedings of the day."[74] The Central Society soon settled down into
an organized routine: rooms were secured at 19 Old Bond Street; a secretary was appointed; and office hours set from ten to four.[75]

The organ of the Anti-Corn-Law League, The League, frequently as-
serted that the newly formed protectionist society ought more properly be
called the Rent Protection Society for its main purpose was to protect

landlords, not tenants. "The farmers," it wrote, "are merely made the stalking-horses behind which the landlords seek to maintain the monopoly they believe so essential to their own interests and their power...."[76] There may be some truth in this charge, but it must be remembered that Baker and the Essex farmers had initiated the movement: the landlords made the overtures for merging. Furthermore, as we shall see, the Central Society was not the most active force in the protectionist movement. Protection's real strength lay in the local societies scattered throughout the country and here farmers were able to exert significant influence. A reading of the accounts of numerous agricultural protectionist meetings held during the first months of 1844--as reported in The Times, the Morning Post, and local newspapers such as the Essex Standard, Lincolnshire Chronicle, and Bucks Herald--reveals the prominence of farmers at those meetings.[77]

Throughout 1844 the Anti-League (as it came to be known) continued to grow. One Conservative journal, the John Bull, reported nearly 100 societies in England by March, 1844.[78] The Morning Post cited the size and scope of the societies as "proofs" of the establishment of a "great Country Party...."[79] It was reported that there were twenty local protectionist societies in Lincolnshire alone.[80] As one rural Lincolnshire observer wrote in January, 1844: "I am glad to see that the agriculturists throughout Lincolnshire are now aware of the danger they stand in from Mr. Cobden and the "League." Meetings of Farmers are being held in a great many different towns in this County."[81]

Apart from passing resolutions against the League, the Anti-League did little else in 1844. There were two reasons for this restricted activity. First, there was some indecision as to what further action could be taken.

The Duke of Richmond was emphatic against any participation in political matters including electioneering--much to the disappointment of some of his followers.[82] Secondly, the threat to protection seemed to recede in 1844. Parliamentary attention was absorbed by the passage of the Factory Act, the Bank Charter Act, and the Companies Act--further examples of Peel's administrative and social reforms. The only debate of consequence to the protectionists was that on Villiers' annual free trade motion, which predictably failed to carry.[83]

Events took a different turn in 1845, however. Peel's budget for that year, introduced in February, continued the trend of his 1842 budget by striking off a further 430 articles from the tariff list and reducing duties on other articles. Although agricultural products were generally unaffected, it seemed an ominous sign to the protectionist. In late 1845 events in Ireland convinced Peel that further changes in the Corn Laws were necessary. Disturbing reports of a massive potato crop failure in Ireland raised fears of famine. To insure adequate grain supplies, Peel decided to suspend the Corn Laws. But he realized that once remitted temporarily, corn duties could never be reimposed.[84] In emergency Cabinet sessions in November and early December, 1845 Peel argued, in vain, for his policy: only three Cabinet members supported him. Matters were complicated when on November 22 Lord John Russell made public his conversion to free trade in a dramatic letter to the electors of London. Prior to this declaration Lord John had been a supporter of at least a protective minimum for corn in the form of a low fixed duty. The political effect of Lord John's letter was to consolidate Cabinet support for Peel. All but Lord Stanley and the Duke of Buccleuch now sided with Peel. Peel doubted, however, that he could carry the alteration of the corn laws through parliament if his cabinet were not united. Therefore he resigned on December 5. During the next two weeks Lord John attempted to form a ministry, but because of Whig divisions he was unable to do so. On December 20 Peel returned to office.

The affair made it clear that Peel's was the only government that could then be formed thus strengthening his hand for the struggle to come. It also further excited the already edgy protectionists. It was widely suspected in protectionist circles that Peel would now drastically alter the Corn Law. At the Anti-League's Central Society meeting in London in December, 1845, protectionist suspicion of Peel's intentions prompted a change of policy.[85] In a speech before the Society, the Duke of Richmond reminded those in attendance that at the last annual meeting it had been decided not to agitate in the country for the aims of the Society: "He had always felt, as farmers, they ought not to endeavour to set man against man...." Now, however, Richmond said, that must change: the protectionist societies throughout the country "ought to be up and doing." It was decided to send a circular to every local association to inform them of a special meeting of the Central Society for January 12, 1846, the purpose of which was to rescind the fourth rule of the Society which prohibited any political activity or electioneering among its members. At the meeting on the twelfth, the fourth rule of the Society, "That the Society, shall, on no account, interfere in any election for a Member to serve in Parliament," was expunged. In its place, a general resolution was passed: "That the Society is most anxious to impress upon the local Protection Societies the necessity of supporting, in the event of an election, only those candidates who steadily maintain the present amount of protection, without political bias or party feeling."[86]

There is some indication that even before Richmond's statement—and perhaps against his wishes—a few protectionist societies had been engaged in the registration of county voters. They had also engaged solicitors to represent them in the registry courts to object to certain electors (presumably free traders) at the annual revision of the registers.[87] This was in response to the registration and objection activities of the League which had undertaken the creation of county votes on an unprecedented scale in an attempt to win county seats for free trade candidates.[88]

The new political activism of the Anti-League was evident during the first weeks of 1846. Over thirty local associations met during January and early February, 1846.[89] In some cases direct pressure on MP's was decided at these meetings. The Northamptonshire Protection Society sent a deputation of three to W. R. Cartwright, MP for South Northamptonshire, to urge him, if his views differed from theirs on the Corn Law, to resign.[90] The Cambridgeshire Society passed a resolution pledging electoral loyalty only to parliamentary members supporting protection.[91] At the Nottinghamshire South by-election in February, 1846, occasioned by Lord Lincoln's appointment as Chief Secretary to Ireland, protectionists helped elect Thomas Hildyard. The Anti-League contributed ₤2000 to the campaign and one of its most experienced election agents.[92] When R. H. Clive, MP for South Shropshire, announced at the Shropshire Agricultural Protection Society that he would go with Peel, he was greeted with cries of "Resign! Resign!" from the audience.[93] The Buckingham Agricultural Protection Society at its December 31, 1845, meeting formed a committee to interview borough and county members and, if they were unsound on protection, to ask for their resignation.[94]

Sir Thomas Fremantle, MP for Buckingham, who was then serving as Chief
Secretary for Ireland, felt that he could not uphold protection in the
light of his experiences in Ireland and complied with the resignation
request.[95] Lord Ashley, MP for Dorset, after characteristically confiding
to his diary for weeks beforehand his agonized indecision, finally resigned over the protection issue on January 31.[96] Protectionist demands on
parliamentary representatives were taking their toll, as Peel himself ack-
nowledged in a letter to his brother in late January: "We are in a great
turmoil here about resignations. Many...talk of resigning their seats.
They feel they cannot conscientiously vote against me, yet are inclined
either to give up Parliament, or to pass through the ordeal of reelection"[97]
Of twenty-four by-elections held in early 1846, sixteen were won by
protectionists.[98]

     Because of their disenchantment with Peel and the Conservative leader-
ship and the impossibility of turning to the Whigs, many farmers and gentry
gave voice at local Anti-League meetings to the idea of forming another
party based on protectionist principles. At the Horncastle Agricultural
Protection Society's meeting in early January, Mr. J. Ellwood of Mareham
declared that: "This was no time to talk about Whiggism and Toryism;
another ism was rising up,--free-trade-ism which threateded to swallow up
both the others."[99] At the Lincoln and Lindsey Agricultural Protection
Society meeting about the same time, R. A. Christopher, MP for Lindsey,
pledged himself to stand "aloof from all party or faction" in the House of
Commons and to "range himself with those members who would form what might
be called the country party in the house..."[100] At a meeting in December,
1845, of the Essex Agricultural Protection Society, Robert Baker, founder of

the Anti-League, declared that the question before the country "was not a question of politics—of whether its advocates were Whigs or Tories—of whether a Peel or a Russell were to hold the reins of government: it was a question of protection or not protection...."[101] The Essex Standard summed up the feeling thus: "We must...in future discard the old distinctions of party: these have become obsolete. We are not in this question Tories, Conservatives, Whigs, or Radicals any longer, but we are now divided into Protectionists and Leaguers."[102]

Peel's parliamentary speech of January 27, 1846, confirmed every protectionist fear. "I am about to proceed on the assumption," Peel told an expectant House, "that the repeal of prohibitory and the relaxation of protective duties is in itself a wise principle. I am about to proceed on the assumption that protective duties, abstractedly and on principle, are open to objection...."[103] He proposed the repeal not only of the Corn Laws but of tariffs on imported articles generally. To ease the shock he suggested a gradual diminution of duties over the next three years until final abolition on February 1, 1849. Hoping to divert agricultural criticism, Peel also proposed that the Treasury assume the cost of several social services previously born by the counties—the highway rate, maintenance of prisoners, half of the medical relief afforded by poor law relief, and the expense of auditors of poor law unions. The law of settlement would also be charged to alleviate claims made on rural areas by those on poor relief.[104]

If Peel had hoped these sweeteners to the agricultural interest would mitigate criticism, he was mistaken. In the weeks to follow, debating time on the Corn Law was largely taken up by attacks on Peel and his policy by members of his own party: rarely did Whig or Radical speakers have the floor.

The first day's debate, following Peel's introduction of Corn Law repeal, was typical. Feelings were high as pent-up frustration erupted among constituency-battered backbenchers. The Earl of March, member for West Sussex, declared himself "horrified, distressed...astonished" at Peel's proposals.[105] Col. Sibthorp, member for Lincoln, declared Peel's speech "odious" and thought its content "was such as to excite the disgust and indignation of the British public.[106] Sir John Tyrell, member for North Essex, said he felt "as he imagined persons would have felt in the Peninsular war, if the Duke of Wellington and the greater part of his staff had gone over to Marshal Soult." He was also fearful that the Whigs would now join with Peel "for the purpose of drawing the agricultural Members through the utmost possible quantity of dirt."[107]

During the course of the debate protectionist MPs stressed the damage to farmers if the Corn Laws were abolished. H. T. Liddell, member for Durham, spoke for many when he stated that in the north of England there had been "an unbounded improvement" in agriculture: "miles and miles" of drain tiles had been laid down. But all of this was based on continued protection from foreign agriculture.[108] George Bankes, member for Dorsetshire, claimed that repeal would not harm landlords so much as their tenants. He predicted that the "whole class" of tenants would be "swept away" if repeal passed.[109] A. S. O'Brien, member for North Northamptonshire, in what was generally regarded as one of the best speeches on the protectionist side, claimed the whole question of protection was largely a tenants' question. Smaller tenants, especially, could not withstand the increased competition that repeal would mean. "We will not aid you in your triumph over these poor men," O'Brien promised Peel. "We do not envy you the victory you seek to achieve over them. In that triumph we refuse to participate. We may be small in number and uninfluential in debate, but we will raise our voices against the injustice which we may be unable to avert."[110]

Protectionists charged Peel with inconsistency, amplified by the more extreme protectionists to charges of political treachery. Most often sounding this theme was Lord George Bentinck, member for King's Lynn. Bentinck's role in the Corn Laws debate was curious and unexpected. He had scarcely spoken a word in the House in eighteen years and was much better known as a sportsman, often wearing a scarlet hunting coat to parliamentary sittings.[111] Although he had been a loyal follower of Peel in the past, the prospect of Peel's desertion to the ranks of the free traders was too much for his simply held rural beliefs. On February 27, 1846, the twelfth night of debate, Lord George made the first of his many speeches. In it he deplored not so much the abolition of protection as the conduct of Peel. The "proud aristocracy" (by which he seemed to mean the protectionist aristocracy), he declared, "never have been guilty, and never can be guilty, of double-dealing with the farmers of England--of swindling our opponents, deceiving our friends, or betraying our constitutents."[112]

The charge of Peel's treachery and party desertion was most eloquently set out by Bentinck's improbable colleague, Benjamin Disraeli. In a speech on February 20, 1846, Disraeli explained the protectionist view. "We do not complain of the right hon. Baronet for having changed his opinion...but that he has outraged public opinion--that he has prevented its legitimate action in the settlement of questions by the aid of party, or embodied public opinion...."[113] Had Lord John Russell brought forward free trade in corn, Disraeli continued, that would have been a legitimate use of party

and public opinion. But Peel had sworn to uphold the Corn Laws; now he
proposed their repeal. And, moreover, he did so without consulting the
electorate. Disraeli's remarks had point. Peel had shown himself insen-
sitive to the opinions of a large percentage of the Conservative electorate and he had done little to prepare the agricultural members for repeal.
Peel was never a sound party man; he regarded himself as a national leader above party. His disregard for the electoral bonds that existed between the electorate and their representatives was his most serious mis-
take during the Corn Law controversy of 1846.

The protectionist arguments were stated again and again in the House
of Commons from late January through mid-May. In an attempt to delay the
proceedings the protectionists adopted filibustering tactics. Lord George
Bentinck was most conspicuous although his labored presentation of statistics and tables only served to tire and alienate the House. Occasional
flashes of eloquence from O'Brien or Disraeli were the few saving graces on
the protectionist side. Still, the protectionist opposition was, in Greville's words, "plausible and imposing enough," though thin in argumentation
and consisting too often of vindictive anti-Peelite statements culminating
in Disraeli's famous attack on Peel during the last day of debate.[114] The
final vote in the Commons showed surprising protectionist strength. The
government had 329 votes and the protectionists 231--a difference of only
98. As would be expected members from agricultural regions formed the
majority of the protectionist side. The bill had a relatively easier time
in the House of Lords although hints of political betrayal were also heard
in that chamber. The bill was given its third reading in the House of
Lords on June 25, 1846. That same day Peel was defeated in the House of

Commons on the Irish Coercion Bill by a combination of Whigs, Radicals,
Irish members, and protectionists. Four days later he resigned, never
again to hold office.

With their defeat in 1846, farmers' disillusionment with the Conservative leadership reached a climax. A bond of loyalty had been broken.
No less keen a disappointment for farmers was the abandonment of protection by many of the aristocracy who had been the traditional supporters
of the land. The reaction among farmers to this desertion by some of
their traditional and political leaders led to the formation of a country
party with its own leadership and party platform. It has rightfully been
called the Protectionist Party, and it is the subject of the following
chapter.

Footnotes to Chapter V

[1]Essex Std., Feb. 22, 1839.

[2]The Times, July 6, 1841.

[3]Annual Register, 1841, p. 147, from which the following election statistics are also taken.

[4]For a useful discussion of the election, see Betty Kemp, "The General Election of 1841," History, vol. XXXVIII, no. 130 (June, 1952), pp. 146-57.

[5]Annual Register, 1841, p. 144.

[6]Essex Std., May 21, 1841.

[7]Ibid., June 25, 1841.

[8]Lincolnshire Chr., June 11, 1841.

[9]Olney, Lincolnshire Politics, pp. 111-15. Handley's name was placed in nomination without his knowledge. This accounts for his apparent candidacy in the poll book.

[10]Ibid., May 14, 1841.

[11]Hansard, 3rd ser., vol. 58, May 27, 1841, 830.

[12]Ibid., 834. Worsley's speech of self-defense moved The Times to characterize Worsley as "a slippery Lord" (The Times, May 28, 1841).

[13]The defeated third candidate was the Conservative C. H. Cust, a younger son of Viscount Alford. He was little known in the constituency and an ineffective campaigner. See Olney's discussion of the election in his Lincoonshire Politics, pp. 108-111.

[14] See vol. 1 of William Marshall, _Rural Economy of the West of England_ (London, 1796). The Board of Agriculture's report for 1811 agreed with Marshall's evaluation, characterizing the general course of crops as "extremely reprehensilbe" (G.B. Worgan, _General View of the Agriculture of the County of Cornwall_ (London, 1811), p. 55). An earlier Board of Agriculture's report recorded its author's amazement at the lack of basic good husbandry practices; see Robert Fraser, _General View of the County of Cornwall_ (London, 1794), _passim_. See also W.F. Karkeek, "On the Farming of Cornwall," _Jnl. of the Royal Agric. Soc. of England_ (1845), pt. 2, pp. 400-62.

[15] Census of Great Britain, 1851, Population Tables, _Parliamentary Papers_ (1852-53), LXXXVIII, pts. 1 and 2. See the heading "Occupations of the People, Farmers (Acreage and Men)," _passim_.

[16] V.M. Chesher, "Some Cornish Landowners, 1690-1760: A Social and Economic Study," (Oxford thesis, 1957), ch. 1; John Rowe _Cornwall in the Age of the Industrial Revolution_ (Liverpool U. Press, 1953), p. 245.

[17] Peters once described his own farm as employing forty laborers, fourteen women, and thirteen boys (_Royal Corn. Gaz._, Mar. 27, 1830). He started a flock of Leicester sheep in Cornwall as early as 1790 and held regular ram sales until 1840. He was also instrumental in introducing shorthorn cattle into Cornwall (Rowe, _Cornwall in the Age of Industrial Revolution_, pp. 237-8). See also Elvins, "Reform Movement and County Politics in Cornwall," p. 24.

[18]The Conservative organ, the Royal Cornwall Gazette, warned the farmers that the reformers were committed to eventual abolition of the Corn Law. "The course for the farmer is therefore clear; it remains but for him to give his vote for no man who will not pledge himself to oppose any alteration of those laws" (Royal Corn. Gaz., Sept. 22, 1832). For details of the election of 1832 in Cornwall, see Elvins, "Reform Movement and County Politics in Cornwall," ch. VI.

[19]As he stated in an election speech at Camelford in July, 1837 (Royal Corn. Gaz., July 21, 1837).

[20]Elvins, "Reform Movement and County Politics in Cornwall,: ch. VIII.

[21]A sternly religious and staunch Conservative, William Rashleigh, Sr., considered it a landlord's prerogative to control his tenants' voting. See the letters to his agent prior to the elections of 1832 and 1837 in Cornwall R.O., Rashleigh MSS, DDR 5325, Aug. 15, 1832; and DDR 4330, Aug. 14, 1837.

[22]Bucks Her., July 24, 1841.

[23]As reported in the Lincolnshire Chr., July 9, 1841.

[24]The Croker Papers, ed. Louis J. Jennings (New York, 1884), Vol. II, Aug 3, 1842, p. 178.

[25]Ibid., Oct. 30, 1842, p. 183

[26]As he expressed it in a letter to Lord Ripon, President of the Board of Trade (Parker, Peel, Vol. II, Oct. 19, 1841, pp. 496-97).

[27] _Hansard_, 3rd ser., vol. 60, Feb. 9, 1842, 232.

[28] _Ibid._, Feb. 16, 1842, 595.

[29] _Statutes at Large_, vol. XVI, 5 & 6 Victoria, c. 14.

[30] _Hansard_, 3rd ser., vol. 60, Feb. 25, 1842, 1093ff.

[31] _Ibid._, vol. 61, Mar. 9, 1842, 358. Knatchbull's protectionist sentiment was muted by office; at that time, he was serving as Paymaster
General and sat in the Cabinet. Two months later, when Peel's general
tariff reduction was proposed, Knatchbull did register some opposition—
especially to those clauses reducing duties on imported hops and apples.
This was in deference to Kentish hop and fruit growers (Sir Hughe
Knatchbull-Hugessen, _Kentish Family_ (London, 1960), pp. 242-3).

[32] _Hansard_, 3rd ser., vol. 62, Apr. 7, 1842, 33.

[33] _Ibid._, 34.

[34] _Ibid._, 35.

[35] _Ibid._, 40.

[36] Peel Papers, Add MSS 40443, ff. 156-57, March, 1842, Geo. Finch (formerly
M.P. for Stamford, Lincs.) to Capt. E. Savrin, R.N.

[37] _Lincolnshire Chr._, Apr. 8, 1842.

[38] The following account is taken from _Essex Std._, Apr. 22, 1842.

[39] _Bucks Her._, Feb. 26, 1842.

[40] _Royal Corn. Gaz._, Apr. 15, 1842. This instance of protectionist dismay was received gleefully by the Whiggish _West Briton_: "it appears that the farmers in the neighborhood of Callington feel exceedingly sore, that after the exertions they had made to place the Tories in power upon the pledges that they and they alone were the "farmers' friends," the first act of the new government...should be to introduce measures... injurious to agriculture..." (_West Briton_, Apr. 15, 1842).

[41] _Statutes at Large_, vol. XVI, 5 & 6 Victoria, c. 47.

[42] _Hansard_, 3rd ser., vol. 63, May 23, 1842, 618.

[43] _Essex Std._, Oct. 21, 1842.

[44] _Hansard_, 3rd ser., vol. 66, Feb. 16, 1843, 1.

[45] As finally acted into law; see _Statutes at Large_, vol. XVI, 6 & 7 Victoria, c. 29.

[46] _Essex Std._, May 12, 1843.

[47] _Ibid_.

[48] _Lincolnshire Chr._, Apr. 28, 1843.

[49] _Ibid_.

[50] _Ibid_.

[51] _Bucks Her._, Apr. 29, 1843; an account of the meeting was also carried in the _Essex Std._, Apr. 28, 1843.

[52]Lincolnshire Chr., Apr. 28, 1843.

[53]Lincolnshire Chr., May 5, 1843.

[54]Hansard, 3rd ser., vol. 69, May 19, 1843, 577.

[55]Ibid., 579.

[56]Usually a model of comprehensiveness, Barnes, History of the English Corn
Laws, does not discuss the Canadian Corn Bill. A discussion may be
found in R.L. Schuyler, "British Imperial Preference and Sir Robert Peel,"
Pol. Sci. Quarterly, vol. XXXII, no. 3 (Sept., 1917), pp. 429-49.

[57]Ellenborough Papers, P.R.O. 30/12/1/6, f. 631, Mar. 4, 1843

[58]Ibid., f. 27, May 31, 1842.

[59]So wrote Colchester to Ellenborough in a letter the following year
(Ellenborough Papers, P.R.O. 30/12/1/6, f. 67, May 31, 1843).

[60]As C.P. Villiers put it in a letter to Cobden: the farmers were the ones
"really who have the govt. of this country in their hands..." (Norman
McCord, The Anti-Corn Law League (London, 1968), 2nd ed., p. 143).

[61]McCord, Anti-Corn Law League, p. 147.

[62]Essex Std., July 14, 1843.

[63]Ibid., Nov. 17, 1843.

[64]See Baker's testimony to the Select Committee of the House of Lords on the Burdens affecting Real Property, Parliamentary Papers (1846) VI, pt. 1, pp. 21 ff., where he noted that in 1843 he leased 1200 acres.

[65]Essex Std., Dec. 1, 1843.

[66]Ibid., Dec. 29, 1843; see also the account in The Times, Dec. 23, 1843.

[67]The Times, Jan. 8, 1844; Jan. 10, 1844; Jan. 27, 1844; Jan. 31, 1844.

[68]Morning Post, Jan. 18, 1844.

[69]The Spectator, no. 813, Jan. 27, 1844, p. 73.

[70]The Times, Jan. 30, 1844.

[71]Ibid., Feb. 19, 1844.

[72]Ibid., Feb. 21, 1844; Farmers' Mag., vol. IX, March, 1844, pp. 276-77.

[73]The Times, Feb. 21, 1844.

[74]Ibid.

[75]Farmers' Mag., Apr., 1844, vol. IX, p. 472.

[76]The League, no. 23, Mar. 2, 1844, p. 377.

[77]This accords with the view of George L. Mosse, "The Anti-League: 1844-1846," Econ. Hist., Rev., vol. XVII, no. 2 (1947), although Mosse may have put it a bit strongly when he wrote that the landlords were only the "reluctant and timorous followers" of the farmers (p. 134). Mary Lawson-Tancred, "The Anti-League and the Corn Law Crisis of 1846," Hist. Jnl., vol. III, no. 2 (1960) seems to think farmers were less important in the Anti-League than they actually were.

[78]John Bull, Mar. 4, 1844.

[79]Morning Post, Feb. 24, 1844.

[80]The Spectator, no. 823, Apr. 6, 1844, p. 317.

[81]Lincolnshire R.O., 3 Anc 7/23/44/86, George Scott (bailiff to Lord Willoughby) to Lewis Kennedy, Jan. 26, 1844.

[82]See Richmond's speech to the agricultural meeting at Steyning, Sussex, in late January, 1844 (Morning Post, Jan. 30, 1844; also in John Bull, Feb. 3, 1844).

[83]Hansard, 3rd ser., vol. 73, June 26, 1844, 1526.

[84]Parker, Peel, vol. III, Peel to Lord Heytesbury, Oct. 15, 1845, p. 224.

[85]The account of the meeting is taken from The Times, Dec. 10, 1845.

[86]John Bull, Dec. 27, 1845.

[87]See the testimony of William Wilmot, a Conventry solicitor and member of the Warwickshire Association for the Protection of Agriculture, before the Select Committee on Votes of Electors, Parliamentary Papers (1846) VIII, 175 ff.; also the testimony of W.W. Burrell, secretary of the Sussex Agricultural Protection Society (of which Richmond was President) in ibid., pp. 344 ff.; and George Dempster, a Brighton solicitor and member of the Sussex Agricultural Protection Society in ibid., pp. 354 ff.

[88] For a general discussion of the League's electioneering activities, see McCord, Anti-Corn Law League, pp. 148 ff. For a specific example of League tactics, see F.M.L. Thompson, "Whigs and Liberals in the West Riding," Engl. Hist. Rev., vol. LXXIV (1959), pp. 214-239.

[89] See John Bull, Jan. 3, 1846; Jan. 10, 1846; Jan. 17, 1846; Feb. 7, 1846.

[90] Ibid., Feb. 7, 1846.

[91] The Times, Jan. 12, 1846.

[92] Robert Stewart, The Politics of Protection (Cambridge U., 1971), pp. 57-8.

[93] The Times, Feb. 10, 1846.

[94] Bucks Her., Feb. 7, 1846.

[95] Davis, "Study of a "Pocket Borough," Huntington Lib. Quarterly, pp. 176 ff. Lord Chandos, The Duke of Buckingham's son, was returned inopposed in Fremantle's place.

[96] Edwin Hodder, The Life and Work of the Seventh Earl of Shaftesbury, K.G. (London, 1886), vol. II, diary entries from Oct. 25, 1845, pp. 120 ff.

[97] Parker, Peel, Vol. III, Peel to William Peel, Jan. 31, 1846, p. 337.

[98] Wilbur Devereux Jones and Arvel B. Erickson, The Peelites, 1846-1857 (Ohio State, 1972), pp. 18-23.

[99] Lincolnshire Chr., Jan. 9, 1846.

[100] Ibid.

[101] Essex Std., Jan. 2, 1846.

[102] Ibid., Jan. 16, 1846.

[103] Hansard, 3rd ser., vol. 83, Jan. 27, 1846, 239.

[104] See D.C. Moore, "The Corn Laws and High Farming," Econ. Hist. Rev., 2nd ser., vol. XVIII, no. 3 (Dec., 1965), pp. 544-61, for a discussion of Peel's intentions.

[105] Hansard, 3rd serv., vol. 83, Jan. 27, 1846, 311.

[106] Ibid., 310.

[107] Ibid., 306, 307-8.

[108] Ibid., 294.

[109] Ibid., 327.

[110] Ibid., Feb. 10, 1846, 656.

[111] See Benjamin Disraeli, Lord George Bentinck: A Political Biography (London, 1852), for details of Bentinck's life.

[112] Hansard, 3rd ser., vol. 84, Feb. 27, 1846, 349.

[113] Ibid., vol. 83, Feb. 20, 1846, 1319-20.

[114] Greville Memoirs, Second Part, vol. II, Feb. 25, 1846, p. 100. The most telling of Disraeli's remarks--and the high water mark of the protectionist vendetta against Peel--may be found in Hansard, 3rd ser., vol. 86, May 15, 1846, 675 and 676.

Chapter VI--The Protectionist Party

In the three years following Corn Law repeal protection seemed a
lost political cause, both in the countryside and in parliament. In
rural districts rising agricultural prices dampened popular demands
for protectionism. Wheat prices recovered from the lows of the mid-
1840's (when 50s. a quarter was common) to reach 69s. 9d. in 1847.
The result was, as Stanley complained to Croker in mid-1847, that the
farmers were "completely apathetic" about political matters.[1] The
Anti-League became moribund. At the general election of 1847, campaign speeches were less strident than in previous elections. Indeed,
the election as a whole was the calmest since 1832.[2] The election
results reflected electoral indifference. Although some 230 protectionist members were returned to parliament, this was approximately
the same number as before the election. Opposed to the protectionists
and supporting Lord John Russell's Whig government were about 330
liberals of every stripe (including Whigs, Radicals, and Irish members), and 98 free trade Conservatives, or Peelites.[3]

In the years immediately following 1846, the protectionists in
parliament suffered from two severe problems--loss of morale and lack
of leadership. Since most of the Conservative leaders had gone with
Peel the parliamentary protectionists were, as Greville put it,
"ancephalous."[4] Only Stanley, head of the protectionists and leader
in the House of Lords, had administrative experience and national
stature. The position of Lord George Bentinck as leader in the House
of Commons merely exacerbated matters. He was not well suited for
the post. There was little personal cordiality between Stanley and

Bentinck, perhaps because of the latter's intimidating earnestness.
Bentinck was also unpopular among many of the backbench protectionists.
Beneath Bentinck's rough and sporting exterior ran a deep current of
Whig libertarianism. Most particularly, he was not sound on the religious issue. He could not condone the anti-Catholic passions of many
protectionists. Another side of his liberal religious views emerged
after the general election, when Baron Rothschild, the first Jew to
be elected to the House of Commons, was returned for the City of
London. Since Jews could not at that time swear on the oath, Lord
John Russell brought forward a bill that would allow Rothschild to
take his seat. Although the protectionists generally were opposed to
the bill, Bentinck favored it. A few days after his supporting speech
in the House of Commons, he received a letter from the whip, Beresford,
which intimated he must be prepared for dismissal as leader. Bentinck,
tired of the   long internecine struggle, lost patience with the
protectionists and predicted in a letter to Croker that the party was
on the verge of breaking up because of its degeneration into a "No
Popery" and "No Jew" party.[5]

When Bentinck resigned in February, 1848, it provoked a further
crisis in the party. Among protectionists the only other potential
leader in the House of Commons was Benjamin Disraeli. But Disraeli
had also been active in supporting Russell on the Jewish Disabilities
Bill. Clearly the objections to Bentinck applied to Disraeli as well.
The choice finally fell on the Marquis of Granby, eldest son of the
fifth Duke of Rutland. Granby was tall, handsome, amiable ("if these
are qualifications," Greville wrote[6]) and, most important, impeccably
Tory. But his incapacity was clear even to himself; he resigned

within a few weeks. For the remainder of the session of 1848 the protectionists had no official leader in the House of Commons, so that
its affairs had to be managed by Stanley from the House of Lords through
the two whips.[7] Without a recognized leader in the House of Commons
the protectionists sank to their lowest ebb. They were further weakened
by the sudden death of Bentinck, who had remained an active backbencher,
in September, 1848.

Protectionist fortunes, however, soon took a turn for the better.
In 1849, Disraeli became protectionist leader in the House of Commons.
Although backbenchers were unhappy at this prospect, no real alterna-
tive existed. Disraeli was able, ambitious, and a politician of
genius who had served his party well since 1846. A further boost to
the cause of protection was the revival of popular protection under
the stimulus of falling agricultural prices. Wheat prices, which had
already declined from a high of nearly 70s. a quarter in 1847 to 50s.
6d. in 1848, sank to 44s. 3d. in 1849; by 1850 the average was 40s.
3d.[8] England was entering one of her most severe agricultural depressions. Once again, farmers engaged in political activity to seek a
more favorable agricultural policy from the government. Their active
support seemed to promise an increased parliamentary representation
for protectionists in any future election. Indeed, at a series of
by-elections in 1849 protectionists gained seats at Kidderminster,
Reading, South Staffordshire, North Hampshire, and Cork.[9]

The strength of the protectionist revival placed Disraeli in an
awkward position. He was not a confirmed protectionist--as the party
but dimly perceived. His aim as leader was to retain the loyalty of
the party while moving them away from their obsession with protection.

He realized that to advance his party (and himself), he had to widen
its electoral appeal. But with a revival of popular protectionism in
the constituencies, this was not an easy task. Disraeli's course of
action from 1849 to 1852 demonstrates clearly the strength of popular
protectionism as it affected his leadership. Time and again he was
forced by constituency and parliamentary pressures to retreat from
his more advanced views on free trade and to equivocate in his statements of policy.

Disraeli's difficulties were clearly demonstrated in the parliamentary session of 1849. His House of Commons speech of March 8,
1849, marked the first appearance there in nearly three years of a
topic concerning agricultural politics. Although he praised protection as the best commercial policy for Britain, he stated he would
not seek its return. He suggested instead a revision of the financial
charges on land: local taxes and poor rates were special targets.
"After the change of 1846," Disraeli declared, "which so greatly affected the agricultural interest, I think they are entitled at least
to this...."[10]

In the debate that developed during the following week on the
motion, it was obvious that many members of the party were more mili-
tantly protectionist than was Disraeli. William Miles (East Somerset-
shire) and E.S. Cayley (North Riding) were extreme in their statements. Cayley warned that "the House would soon learn, if it per-
severed in an unjust and oppressive course towards the farmers of
England...that it was neither safe nor politic so to treat them."[11]
The Whig government was unmoved, however, and Disraeli's motion lost
by 280 to 189.

Disraeli had already discovered that fervent protectionism in this session was not limited to backbenchers. Lord Stanley, who had resigned from Peel's cabinet in 1845 rather than accept free trade, was as firm a protectionist as any farmer. At the opening of the session on February 1, 1849, Stanley and the protectionist peers in the House of Lords attempted to carry an amendment to the Queen's Speech which would have forced ministerial acknowledgement of the agricultural depression. Drawn up by Stanley, Richmond, Redesdale, and Malmesbury the night before, the motion nearly succeeded, losing by only two votes--52-50.[12] In introducing the amendment, Stanley voiced strong protectionist sentiments. "I am the uncompromising enemy of the miscalled, one-sided, bastard free trade, which has been introduced by the Government for the benefit of foreigners, and to the detriment of British subjects," he declared. "Every day's experience convinces me more and more that this country...must return to the principle of protection."[13] Stanley underscored his public statements to a correspondent later in the session. "I think," he wrote, that "the farmers are right in seeking the restoration of protection; and I hope the landlords, and I believe the country, ere long, will go with them."[14]

As the session progressed, Disraeli's moderate brand of protectionism was increasingly criticized. For example, in a lengthy debate on the state of the nation in July when not once did Disraeli utter the word protection, response among parliamentary protectionists was unfavorable. Stronger views were expressed in the constituencies. An editorial in the Lincolnshire Chronicle put it this way : "There is no use in mincing the matter. Parliament must retrace its steps in spite of Sir Robert Peel's prognostications and Mr. Cobden's professed compensations."[15]   At a well-attended protectionist meeting in Sussex in March, criticism was even less guarded. There, an opponent condemned outright Disraeli's tax and rate reduction scheme as "merely a tub thrown to the whale to put the farmers on a wrong scent" (sic).[16]

To counteract the growing sentiment for extreme protection and to amplify his own substitute program Disraeli began a series of speaking engagements in the countryside after the prorogation of parliament in August. It was a strategy reminiscent of Disraeli's once powerful benefactor, Lord Chandos, but with a wholly different aim in mind--to curtail popular protectionism. His first effort at Aylesbury, Bucks, was not successful. He proposed an involved scheme to aid the landed interest by increasing the land tax, applying the resultant revenue to a sinking fund. The fund would be used for the liquidation of the National Debt which in turn would lower rates of interest, allowing the landed classes to borrow more cheaply.[17]   Upon hearing of Disraeli's scheme, Stanley quashed it by pointing out that an increased land tax was sure to be unpopular in counties where the tax was low.[18]   In accordance with Stanley's suggestion that he publicly explain away his financial scheme, Disraeli spoke at the Hinckford Agricultural and Conservative Club at Castle Hedingham, Essex, in October.[19]   Here, Disraeli made an important modification to his Aylesbury speech. Retaining the idea of a sinking fund, he now proposed that it be created by import duties rather than by land taxes. In well-publicized meetings in Buckinghamshire during November and December, 1849, Disraeli reiterated the need for moderate protective duties.[20]

In his retraction, there is no doubt that Disraeli was bowing to
protectionist pressures. Apart from Stanley's injunctions, Disraeli
was receiving other protectionist advice. Beresford reported in
November, 1849, that protectionist sentiment was increasing and that
the Protectionist party "should work that feeling to the utmost."[21]
The following month, Malmesbury urged Disraeli to "go ding dong with
the word 'Protection' in a general sense, for that word right or wrong,
is the tocsin which our Party as a Party will obey."[22] Not the least
important of the protectionist pressures on Disraeli were those
exerted by farmers during Disraeli's country tour.

By mid-1849 the reviving protectionist sentiment was beginning
to appeal to a wider group than the agricultural interest. This was
evident in the establishment in May, 1849, of the National Association for the Protection of British Industry and Capital. It grew out
of the ruins of the old Anti-League organization of the mid-1840's.
Although its nominal president was the Duke of Richmond, the real
force behind the Association was George Frederick Young. Young was a
wealthy Limehouse shipowner whose interest in protection had been
aroused by the Whig government's attack on the Navigation Laws.[23] In
1848, Henry Labouchere, President of the Board of Trade, had brought
forward a motion for the repeal of the Navigation Laws. During the
course of the debates on the Laws in 1848 and 1849, the parliamentary
protectionists staunchly opposed their repeal. It seemed to them a
further and more dangerous extension of the principle of free trade.
When the National Association was formed, its immediate purpose was
to support protectionist peers in their opposition to the bill. They
were unsuccessful, however, and the measure became law in June, 1849.

Young was determined to reverse this decision. Apart from guiding the National Association, he was also busy in the countryside speaking at protectionist rallies and attempting to form a coalition of agricultural shippers' interests. Disraeli disapproved strongly of Young's activities; he saw that Young could be a rival for the loyalty of the farmers. On October 19, 1849, Disraeli sent an agitated letter to Young. "Unless the agricultural constituencies (county and borough)," he wrote, "are prevented from running amuck against the financial system of this country, which, out of suffering and sheer spite and vexation, it is not unnatural they should do, it is all over with England as a great free monarchy...."[24] Stanley, however, disagreed with Disraeli's attempt to restrain Young. In a letter to Disraeli dated October 25, 1849, Stanley expressed the fear that Disraeli's rebuke to Young would "create feelings of both discouragement and of dissatisfaction from those whom it is most important that we should continue to conciliate....I am not, for one, prepared to abandon the principle of protective duties...." Stanley believed that "the public mind is beginning to be impressed with the conviction that Free Trade has proved a delusion; and...our clear policy is to seek to encourage this conviction."[25]

Disraeli's major complaint was that the National Association seemed to regard itself as a sovereign power and was not informing the party of its intentions.[26] Matters came to a head in late 1849. At a protectionist meeting in Bromley, Kent, Young criticized Disraeli's sinking fund scheme as of doubtful use to the protectionists.[27] A few days later a letter appeared in The Times, written by one of the most respected protectionist backbenchers, Sir John Tyrell

of Essex. Tyrell was openly critical of Young and praised Disraeli
as someone who deserved the "grateful thanks rather than the sneers
and insinuations of those whose interests he so powerfully defends."[28]
In the meantime negotiations between Young and Disraeli through a
mediator, Beresford, the whip, had begun. As a result, a conciliatory
letter from Young appeared in The Times a few days after Tyrell's
letter. Young, in his letter, emphasized protectionist unity and
maintained that "past trifling differences" were minor ones. But he
reiterated the right of protectionists to agitate. "Our course...out
of the House, will strengthen the hands of our friends within it...."[29]
Apparently Young had agreed to accept Disraeli's leadership and to
keep the party informed of the National Association's plans.[30] In return, Disraeli dropped the sinking fund scheme and also gave his bless-
ing to rural agitation; as he told an agricultural audience in early
December: "I have no hesitation in saying that I wish the farmers of
this country to be stirring--to know their own position--to remember
that they are...the most important portion of that middle class
which...now are mainly to govern the country."[31]

During the winter of 1849-1850 protectionist meetings of every
sort continued to fill the pages of provincial journals. The message
everywhere was the same--a demand for full agricultural protection.
In Devon, a protectionist county meeting drew 7500 in late December.[32]
In Norfolk, Whig farmers reportedly combined with Conservative landowners to request a county meeting to petition for a return of protection.[33] An estimated twenty thousand attended a protectionist
meeting in Lincolnshire in January, 1850.[34]. In the same month, a
serious riot erupted after a protectionist meeting in Stafford.[33] A

free trade crowd of more than 1000 chased farmers to the railroad station after the meeting, stoning the trains that took the farmers back
into the country. A similar incident occurred in Reading, Berkshire,
when free traders attempted to storm the platform at a protectionist
meeting.[36]

The metropolitan newspapers began to take notice of the protectionist agitation. In December, 1849, The Times remarked that: "A
spontaneous _furor_ has seized the whole Protectionist party, and ex-
hibits itself in a thousand maniacal results."[37] Indeed The Times
thought that because of their support for protection the tenant farmers were "the most conspicuous personages of the day...."[38] The
strength of the protectionist reaction was beginning to alarm some
free traders. Greville believed that, should the depression continue,
it could have disastrous social effects. On February 2, 1850, he
wrote in his diary: "...the farmers have been so terrified and excited by their leaders and orators, that there is good reason to
fear,...that they will...break through all the old patriarchal ties,
and go to any lengths which they may fancy they can make instrumental
to their relief."[39] Greville's foreboding had some basis in fact. As
protectionist agitation continued during 1850 and 1851, there were reports of occasional clashes of opinion between landlords and farmers
at country meetings. When Sir Montague Cholmeley, MP for North Lincolnshire, declared at a Lincolnshire plowing match that a return to
protection was a "vain hope," he was challenged by a farmer who declared that protection was both "requisite and necessary."[40] As Lord

Eglinton explained it to Malmesbury, "in many parts of Scotland, as in England, the farmers think us too lukewarm, and accuse the landlords of deserting them."[41]

Most alarming of all to the defenders of traditional deferential politics were growing manifestations of an independent electoral spirit among farmers. Talk among farmers stressed the need for farmers' representatives to parliament. There was even a report that a national fund was to be established to send farmers to parliament, but this seems to have been abortive.[42] In February, 1851, occurred a startling example of farmers' electoral independence. It was occasioned by the resignation of the sitting member for South Nottinghamshire in December, 1850, for reasons of ill health.[43] A young nobleman, Lord Newark, immediately announced his candidacy; he was the obvious nominee of his father, Lord Manvers, a dominant influence in the county. However, a farmers' candidate, William Barrow, was offered in opposition to Newark. A retired solicitor and experienced magistrate, he was long active in farmers' clubs. The local grandees were reportedly indignant at this intrusion, but Barrow was not intimidated. The campaign soon attracted national attention. The Times wrote of it thus: "A contest of an unprecedented nature is now raging in South Notts.... The tenant-farmers of South Notts have somehow arrived at the conclusion that their cause has not prospered in aristocratical hands, that lords and country gentlemen have too many interests of their own to promote, and that they ought to have a representative of their own instead of a landlords' nominee."[42] As the campaign lengthened, it was reported that Newark's election expenses

were soaring whereas Barrow's remained light since most of his
agents were volunteers.

Little difference could be detected between the candidates' plat-
forms: both were protectionists. The farmers simply wanted their own
candidate. As one of Barrow's supporters put in on nomination day,
Barrow had given "pretty nearly, his whole time to the business of the
county....They wanted for representatives, men of business habits,--
practical men, men acquainted with the operation of laws which they
were called upon to alter or repeal."[45] Another Barrow supporter reminded the election crowd of the unhappy experience in 1846 when some
landlord nominees had voted for Corn Law repeal. Consequently, he
said, the farmers were justifiably suspicious of nominees, who, in
times past, had "always betrayed and deserted them (cheers) . The
farmer had found out, that if he was ever to receive any assistance,
to make any impression on the legislature, he must help himself...."[46]
The contest had been widely reported and its outcome eagerly antici-
pated. The result of the election was very close. Out of nearly 3000
electors polled, Barrow won by a majority of only fifteen votes. The
fact of a farmers' candidate winning in a direct contest over aristocratic influence was, as The Times noted, "truly marvellous."[47]

As popular protectionism increased its hold on the countryside,
the protectionist party consolidated its strength in the House of Commons. During the session of 1850, Disraeli's motion on the equaliza-
tion of the poor rates attracted the largest number of protectionist
supporters ever: the motion was lost only by the narrow margin of
273 to 252.[48] Protectionists found events even more favorable in 1851.
The government coalition of Whigs, Radicals, Irish members, and

Peelites, suffering the usual fate of governmental coalitions, was becoming unmanageable. Early in 1851 a serious political miscalculation
by Lord John, wholly unrelated to agricultural politics, further undermined the coalition and nearly cost him the government. Prior to the
session, word had been received in England that Pope Pius IX had decided to re-establish the Catholic hierarchy in England which had been
abolished in the sixteenth century. Twelve suffragan bishops, headed
by an Archbishop of Westminster, were created. Shortly afterward,
Wiseman, the Archbishop, received a cardinal's hat. A spontaneous
outburst arose against the papacy for this intrusion into a protestant
country. Responding to popular opinion Lord John wrote a letter on
November 4 to the Whig Bishop of Durham denouncing the papacy. Lord
John's public epistle was followed by the government's proposal to
prohibit English Catholic bishops from using the religious titles con-
ferred on them by the papacy. Embodied in the Ecclesiastical Titles
Bill, the proposal was introduced in February, 1851, and passed in
July.

Lord John's motives were unclear in the whole episode. Perhaps
he hoped to capitalize on the protestantism of the countryside to
strengthen his government. Or perhaps he was simply, as Disraeli put
it, "indulging in his hereditary foible--to wit, having a shy at the
Papists...."[49] Whatever his reason, the political cost to Lord John
was high. During the months of debate on the Ecclesiastical Titles
Bill, Lord John steadily lost ground among his Irish allies, many of
whom were Catholic or represented largely Catholic constituencies.
The protectionist opposition was the direct beneficiary of the Irish
defection. Throughout the 1851 session the Irish supported the

protectionists in such numbers as to threaten the existence of the
Whig government. Indeed, Irish anger at Lord John was evident in the
first days of the session. When, in a speech before the House of
Commons on February 11, 1851, Disraeli requested the Whigs to introduce "without delay" some measure for the relief of agriculture, the
Irish were quick to voice their support.[50] Of those Irish members
present and voting, forty-five supported Disraeli's motion and only
twenty-eight voted for Russell. The result was a near victory for
the opposition, Disraeli's motion losing by only 281 to 267.[51] The
majority of only fourteen presaged an acutal defeat of the government a week later when a Radical motion to equalize the borough and
county franchise was passed over Russell's objections. On February
21, therefore, the Whig government resigned.

For five days the protectionists attempted to form an administration. The protectionists were well aware that they were short of
administrative ability and that it would be necessary to include men
from outside their ranks. But approaches made to men of talent among
the Peelites revealed that protection was the bar to office. Of more
consequence was the lack of enthusiasm for office among protectionists too conscious of their lack of ability to serve in high government positions.[52] It was soon obvious that the protectionists could
not form a ministry. On February 27, Lord John resumed office.

This abortive attempt at government was decisive to the fortunes of the Protectionist Party. The proximity of office inclined
many parliamentary protectionists to re-think their fidelity to protection. It was obvious that office would be impossible unless protectionist demands were modified. As Disraeli wrote after the event:

"every public man of experience and influence, however slight, had declined to act unless the principle of Protection were unequivocably renounced."[53] Only a public acceptance of free trade could pave the way to office for the protectionists. Such apostasy would never be accepted, however, by the rural constituencies as Disraeli well knew. The farmers were as firmly protectionist as ever. During the parliamentary recess of 1851, therefore, Disraeli sought once again to moderate protectionist feeling in the constituencies. In two important speeches in Buckinghamshire Disraeli set out his views to the farmers and to the nation at large. In September, 1851, he warned the Royal Bucks Agricultural Association that protection could "never be brought back unless it [was] the interest of all classes" to do so.[54] In a speech at the Royal South Bucks Agricultural Association a few weeks later he emphasized that protection would "never be restored for the farmers alone...."[55] Thus, although he did not abandon the hope of restoring protection, Disraeli hedged its return with a severe qualification: a protective duty must be acceptable to all classes--not merely farmers. To dash completely farmers' hopes for some form of specific agricultural relief, however, would have been electoral suicide. As a substitute for protection Disraeli reiterated his program of tax reduction for the landed classes.

Disraeli's lead in attempting to re-shape constituency opinion was followed by others. William Beresford, M.P. for North Essex, for example, formerly a rabid protectionist and party whip, now adopted a position of studied ambiguity. His speech to the Hinckford (Essex) Agricultural and Conservative Club in October, 1851,

might be taken as a model of political equivocation. Addressing the
Club, Beresford praised protective duties as "wise and just" and assured his audience that he would always seek justice for them "in
every imaginable way that it could be obtained." But he also informed them that "he neither expected to restore, nor cherished the
secret hope of being able to restore" protective duties.[56] Such
statements from the protectionist leadership naturally caused dismay
among the farmers. Their feelings were well expressed by Edward
Ball, a farmer of Burwell, Cambridgeshire, in a speech before the
December, 1851, meeting of the National Association. The recent pro-
nouncements, he said, especially Disraeli's, were "without question,
calculated to produce in the friends of protection an ambiguous, uncertain, and wavering policy."[57]

Disraeli, however, had one great advantage over his militant
protectionist critics: he was now the indisputable protectionist
leader in the House of Commons. His position as leader had been
consolidated during the previous two parliamentary sessions and he
had won the respect, if not the trust, of even the most obstinate
backbencher. If the protectionists were to obtain office, it must be
with Disraeli. As the staunchly protectionist Bucks Herald put it:
"if ever disunion was fatal it is so now. Most earnestly, therefore,
do we entreat the tenants to accept in fairness and sincerity Mr.
Disraeli's intentions towards them...."[58] It was probably felt by
most protectionists in the countryside that Disraeli's lukewarm protection could be sufficiently gingered by Stanley, who had not
moderated his stand.

While the protectionists sought to place themselves in a better bargaining position for office, Lord John's ministry continued to decline. It was fatally weakened when Lord John dismissed Lord Palmerston from the foreign office prior to the session of 1852. Palmerston was a dangerous man to antagonize as Lord John soon discovered. Early in the session of 1852, on February 20, a combination of protectionists, Irish members, and the revengeful Palmerston defeated the government on a relatively minor issue, the reorganization of the local militia. Since Lord John had made the issue a question of confidence, the government resigned. The protectionists had their second chance within a year to form a ministry. This time they succeeded.

As expected, the new government was neither distinguished nor experienced.[59] The cabinet, which contained only three previous office holders, was nicknamed the "Who?Who? Cabinet" because of the aged (and deaf) Duke of Wellington's audible queries when the unfamiliar names were repeatedly told to him in the House of Lords. Stanley, who had succeeded to the earldom of Derby in June, 1851, became First Lord of the Treasury and head of the government. To the general consternation (including his own), Disraeli was made Chancellor of the Exchequer.[60] Familiar names in the protectionist pantheon filled various other offices. Lord John Manners (MP for Colchester) was made First Commissioner of Works and Public Buildings; the former whip, William Beresford (MP for North Essex) was made Secretary at War; R.A. Christopher (MP for North Lincolnshire) became Chancellor of the Duchy of Lancaster; Augustus Stafford (North Norhamptonshire) was made Secretary of the Admiralty;[61] the Marquis of Chandos (MP for Buckinghamshire and son of the ill-fated farmers'

leader of the 1830's) was a Lord of the Treasury; Sir John Trollope
(MP for South Lincolnshire) became Chief Poor Law Commissioner.

The greatest difficulty before the new ministry was the maintenance of its integrity as a protectionist government in the face of
a larger free trade opposition: the ministry could not forsake protection for fear of losing agricultural support, yet it could not
maintain itself in power for long in a predominantly free trade House
of Commons without some sign of commercial liberalism. Cobden, for
example, was determined at the outset either to force from the government a disavowal of protectionist views, or to break them. "We must
challenge to instant combat," he wrote on the formation of the new
ministry.[62] The protectionist response to this dilemma was to follow
an equivocal policy. In his first ministerial statement, even Lord
Derby, who was certainly more protectionist than Disraeli, did not
pledge a return to protection. Instead, he declared that the government would not act on protection until "public opinion should be de-
cidedly and emphatically expressed."[63] His position was that the
government would not take a stand on protection until after the forthcoming general election. If at that time the protectionists received
a majority, some form of protection would be introduced. Should the
protectionists not receive a majority, the implication was that the
Derby ministry would nevertheless attempt to govern though without
a protectionist platform. This policy was very obviously designed to
allow the protectionists to remain in power at any cost, even at the
expense of sacrificing their ostensible political raison d'être.

As Chancellor of the Exchequer, Disraeli hoped to accomplish what his role as opposition leader did not allow--the weaning of farmers from protection. On April 30, 1852, he introduced a provisional budget that reviewed in favorable terms the past ten years of commercial progress under free trade. Disraeli noted that in every year since 1842 there had been reductions in import duties and that it would be "presumptuous" to reverse this trend.[64] The tenor of the speech greatly pleased the free trade opposition. One free trader, T. Wakely of Finsbury, praised Disraeli's speech as an admission that the protectionist had been wrong all along.[65] Not surprisingly, the more militant protectionists were distraught. Expressing "considerable disappointment," Col. Sibthorp (Lincoln) stated that although he would not quite say the speech "amounted to a positive breach of faith,...he felt called on to protest against it."[66] Derby, too, felt that Disraeli had gone too far. As soon as he heard of the speech, he penned 1400 words of protest to Disraeli expressing his "apprehensions" and "anxiety" as to its consequence.[67] Disraeli was forced to retreat. Within a week of his budget speech, he made a short statement in the House of Commons which sabotaged its free trade tenor.[68] It seemed that a previous characterization of the government as "the adventures of a Ministry in search of a policy" was still applicable.[69]

Within a month of Disraeli's budget speech came the test at the polls for the protectionist ministry. There were two major issues during the campaign--protection and protestantism. The religious issue, exacerbated by Lord John's no-popery cry in 1851, still had impact. The protectionists tried to turn it to their advantage by suggesting

that protectionists were the truer protestants. Dark hints of in-
fidelity were cast on some Whig candidates.[70] The more important issue, however, was the determination of the shape of Britain's commercial policy: should the country retain or repudiate free-trade?
The election results were indecisive. Indeed, the campaign itself
was indecisive since the protectionist strategy was designed to ob-
fuscate the issue. The lead was given by Disraeli. His election
address, although it again substituted tax revision for protection as
an aid to the farmer, was yet ambiguous enough to allow room for
doubt.[71] Nor did Derby clarify protectionist policy during the campaign. The lack of a clear electoral platform was indicative of the
lack of unanimity within protectionist ranks. The cabinet members
Herries and Henley opposed Disraeli's election address: Herries advocated a stronger protestant and protectionist line, while Henley opposed Disraeli's "issuing manifestoes in the name of the whole...."[72]

Campaigns throughout England reflected the divided leadership.
Sir John Tyrell of Essex, for example, did not promise a return to
protection: he promised only that the Derby-Disraeli government would
"do what they could" for the farmers.[73] In Lincolnshire, R.A.
Christopher (a cabinet minister and hence speaking with some authority)
declared on nomination day that "it would be no easy matter for the
Government" to restore protection.[74] Other candidates, however, were
much firmer in their advocacy of protection. These were the farmers'
candidates. As early as March, 1851, a meeting of North Lincolnshire
farmers--perhaps inspired by the recently concluded South Notts by-
election--selected a candidate to represent them at any forthcoming
election.[75] They chose the nephew of the protectionist Earl Stanhope,

John Bankes Stanhope, a country gentleman of Revesby Abbey. He announced his candidacy officially as early as August, 1851.[76] Stanhope had been active in local protection societies, and these provided a basis of support once the campaign was underway. Beginning in January, 1852, Stanhope visited farmers' ordinaries to generate further support. In coalition with Stanhope was R.A. Christopher, serving as Chancellor of the Duchy of Lancaster in the Protectionist Ministry. Their opponent was Sir Montague Cholmeley, a Whig who was not strong on protection. The outcome was predictable. As the pollbook indicates, farmers voted heavily for the two protectionists—more than two to one—over the Whig candidate.[77]

Farmer-supported protectionists enjoyed other successes as well. In Herefordshire, farmers and small proprietors were instrumental in returning three protectionists for that county.[78] In Cambridgeshire, the Cambridgeshire Farmers' Association put forward and helped elect Edward Ball of Burwell, a farmer and previously noted critic of Disraeli.[79] In Berkshire, farmers forced out of parliament one of the most distinguished agriculturists of the day. He was Philip Pusey, MP for Berkshire from 1832 to 1852, editor of the Journal of the Royal Agricultural Society, and twice president of the Royal Agricultural Society. Pusey had publicly announced his disavowal of protection the previous year. Consequently the Berkshire Protection Association put up a candidate, of their own, who was ultimately successful.[80]

In the West Country, too, farmers agitated for their own candidates. East Cornish farmers found their man in Nicholas Kendall of Pelyn. Owner of more than 2,000 acres, Kendall was a member of an ancient family said to have sent more representatives to parliament

than any other family in the kingdom.[81] From the mid-1840's Kendall
had been conspicuous at rural gatherings. He was president of the
Lostwithiel Agricultural Association in 1845, presided at the Trigg
Agricultural Society's meeting in 1847, and was known for his out-
spoken views defending the farmer. At the Cornwall Agricultural Association's meeting in 1850, for example, he complained of landlord
indifference to the farmer. Declaring that farmers "had taken their
estates on the faith of a protective duty being continued," he placed
himself squarely in the protectionist camp.[82] Kendall's popularity
among farmers was exemplified by the reception given him at the East
Cornwall Agricultural Association's meeting in May, 1851, where the
applause and cheers which greeted his arrival there provided a "stun-
ning welcome."[83] Kendall's association with Cornish farmers was further underscored at a dinner given him in March, 1852. Sponsored by
the East Cornwall Society for the Protection of Native Industry, the
meeting heard its chairman Robert Taylor, a farmer, urge Cornish
farmers to participate in the forthcoming elections. "We are taking
on ourselves that which was never done in the County of Cornwall before," Taylor declared, "that is, the yeomanry stepping forward and
saying 'We consider ourselves in that position that, as the gentlemen
did not put forward a proper person as representative at former elections, we will not submit to that system,--we will have our own.'"[84]

In spite of the best efforts of protectionist farmers, the party
did not capture a majority of seats. Nevertheless, it did surprisingly
well: the protectionists emerged as the largest party in parliament.[85]
One might guess that Disraeli was not unhappy with this state of affairs. By picking up some seats the credibility of the government

was enhanced, yet not enough was gained to justify the introduction
of a protectionist measure. The indecisive election dictated essentially a <u>status quo ante bellum</u> in the House of Commons. The divided
protectionist leadership had to continue an equivocal commercial
policy while the opposition was determined to force either an affirmation
of free trade or the government's resignation.[86] Pressing their advantage, the freetraders, with C.P. Villiers as spokesman, moved a resolution in the House of Commons in the second week of the new session which declared the repeal of the Corn Laws in 1846 a "wise, just,
and beneficial" measure.[87] The motion was well designed to place the
government in an embarrasing position. If the government voted against
the resolution, it might find itself in a minority and its prestige
perhaps fatally damaged. But if the government voted for the resolution, it would offend its protectionist supporters. A compromise motion offered by Lord Palmerston--who, with others, wished the government a longer life--saved the government.[88] Although free trade in
intent, Palmerston's motion omitted any laudable references to 1846;
it simply declared that the existing commercial system ought to be
maintained and "prudently" extended.[89] On November 26, Villiers' motion was lost, 336 to 256, while Palmerston's passed 468 to 53.

The vote for Palmerston's motion revealed the division within
protectionist ranks. A minority of fifty-three had voted against
Disraeli and the main body of protectionists. Most of this minority
were members of agricultural constituencies and included the farmers'
candidates Ball, Kendall, Stanhope, and Vansittart. They were strongly conscious of the wishes of their constituents on the Palmerston
motion. In his maiden speech Stanhope had declared his opposition to

the motion in accordance "with his duty to his constituents as tenant-farmers...."[90] Of the majority protectionists who had supported the motion, some, at least, did so with uneasy consciences--as a public letter to The Times from E.S. Cayley indicated. Attempting to justify his vote to his constituents, Cayley maintained the Villiers motion was designed only to make the protectionists "eat dirt."[91] Admitting that the Palmerston motion was only slightly less offensive, Cayley had supported it because "the memory of that cause" he had "so long served...could suffer nothing now by a candid acknowledgement of defeat."

Disraeli was not unaware of the reluctant protectionist vote on the Palmerston motion. He was also aware of the dangers of alienating country support. To propitiate the farmers, he offered a program of substantial tax revision in their favor. In a famous five-hour budget speech on December 3, 1852, he proposed halving both the malt and hop taxes; reducing the rate of income tax on farm income from 7d. in the pound to 5½d. in the pound; and reducing the assessment of farmers' profits for taxing purposes from one-half to one-third of their rental.[92] This was consistent with his frequent advocacy of rural tax reductions as a substitute for protection. To recover the consequent revenue losses, he proposed a large increase in the house tax, which would have affected urban more than rural areas.

Disraeli's attempt to compensate the farmer for the final blasting of his protectionist hopes was not successful, however. A budget that so obviously favored rural over urban interests brought the various liberal factions together for a general attack on Disraeli

178

and the government. After several nights of debate, including a mom-
entous clash between Disraeli and Gladstone on the final night, the
vote went against the budget, 305-286. England's short-lived protectionist ministry was at an end.

Footnotes to Chapter VI

[1] *Croker Papers*, vol. 2, June 7, 1847, p. 309.

[2] As *The Times* wrote of the election: "There is not even what people call a calm before the storm....No one cares for the result" (*The Times*, June 11, 1847).

[3] Due to the breakdown in party allegiance, it is difficult to calculate with precision the relative party strenths after the election. The numbers cited here were calculated by Robert Stewart from Dod's *Electoral Facts*. Se Stewart's *Politics of Protection*, p. 112.

[4] *Greville Memoirs (second part)*, vol. 2, July 13, 1847, p. 239.

[5] *Croker Papers*, vol. 2, Dec. 26, 1847, pp. 254-5.

[6] *Greville Memoirs*, vol. 2, Feb. 8, 1848, p. 262.

[7] Robert Blake, *Disraeli*, (New York 1967), p. 262.

[8] Barnes, *Corn Laws*, p. 298.

[9] Stewart, *Politics of Protection*, p. 143.

[10] *Hansard*, 3rd ser., vol. 103, Mar. 8, 1849, 426.

[11] *Ibid.*, Mar. 15, 1849, 816.

[12] Earl of Malmesbury, _Memoirs of an Ex-Minister: An Autobiography_ (London, 1884), 2nd ed., vol. I, p. 238.

[13] _Hansard_, 3d ser., vol. 102, Feb. 1, 1849, 54 and 55.

[14] Stewart, _Politics of Protection_, p. 156 n.4; letter to E. Yorke, Apr. 17, 1849.

[15] _Lincolnshire Chr._, Mar. 16, 1849.

[16] _The Times_, Mar. 28, 1849.

[17] See Blake, Disraeli, pp. 289-90; and William F. Monypenny and George Buckle, _The Life of Benjamin Disraeli, Earl of Beaconsfield_ (New York, 1914), vol. III, pp. 215-8.

[18] Monypenny and Buckle, _Disraeli_, vol. III, letter from Stanley to Disraeli, Sept. 22, 1849, pp. 215-7.

[19] _Essex Std._, Oct. 12, 1849.

[20] _Bucks Herald_, Nov. 3, 1849; _Bucks Herald_, Dec. 8, 1849; _Essex Std._, Dec. 7, 1849; _The Times_, Nov. 1, 1849; _The Times_, Nov. 2, 1849.

[21] Hughenden MSS, B/III/53, Nov. 9, 1849.

[22] _Ibid._, B/III/69, Dec. 2, 1849.

[23] See Robert Livingston Schuyler, _The Fall of the Old Colonial System: A Study in British Free Trade, 1770-1870_ (New York, 1945), ch. V, "The End of the Old Navigational System."

[24] Monypenny and Buckle, _Disraeli_, vol. III, p. 221.

[25]Ibid., p. 233.

[26]Ibid., as expressed in a letter from Disraeli to his wife, Nov. 15, 1849, p. 230.

[27]The Times, Nov. 19, 1849; Essex Std., Nov. 23, 1849.

[28]The Times, Nov. 24, 1849.

[29]Ibid., Nov. 30, 1849.

[30]Monypenny and Buckle, Disraeli, vol. III, p. 233.

[31]Bucks Her., Dec. 8, 1849; the meeting was at Newport Pagnell.

[32]The Times, Dec. 22, 1849.

[33]Hughenden MSS, B/III/99, Jan. 2, 1850, And. Fontaine to Disraeli.

[34]Lincolnshire Chr., Feb. 1, 1850.

[35]The Times, Jan. 11, 1850.

[36]Bucks Her., Jan. 26, 1850

[37]The Times, Dec. 11, 1849.

[38]Ibid., Dec. 12, 1849.

[39]Greville Memoirs, Vol. 2, Feb. 2, 1850, p. 423.

[40]Lincolnshire Chr., Nov. 1, 1850.

[41]Malmesbury, Autobiography, vol. 1, Eglington to Malmesbury, Nov. 24, 1850, p. 266.

[42]The Times, Sept. 14, 1850.

[43]The following account is based upon articles appearing in The Times from December, 1850, through February, 1851.

[44]The Times, Dec. 23, 1850.

[45]Lincolnshire Chr., Feb. 14, 1851.

[46]Ibid.

[47]The Times, Feb. 17, 1851.

[48]Stewart, Politics of Protection, p. 158.

[49]Blake, Disraeli, p. 300.

[50]Hansard, 3d ser., vol. 114, Feb. 11, 1851, 374ff.

[51]The Irish votes were calculated from the division list in Hansard, 3d ser., vol. 114, Feb. 13, 1851, 604-7. A second important protectionist motion--that the government give "due regard" to British farmers in any tax remission or adjustment--was moved by Disraeli on April 11 (Hansard, 3d ser., Vol. 116, 48ff.). This time the Irish supported Disraeli 47-18, which resulted in a government victory of only 263-250 (calculated from Hansard, 3d. ser., vol. 116, April 11, 1851, 118-21).

[52]See the account in Blake, Disraeli, pp. 301-5.

[53]Quoted in Blake, Disraeli, p. 305.

[54]Bucks Her., Sept. 20, 1851.

[55] Ibid., Oct. 11, 1851.

[56] Essex Std., Oct. 10, 1851.

[57] Ibid., Dec. 19, 1851.

[58] Bucks Her., Oct. 11, 1851.

[59] For a complete list of the ministry, see Appendix III.

[60] Blake, Disraeli, p. 311.

[61] In 1847, Augustus Stafford O'Brien changed his name to Augustus O'Brien Stafford (Charles Whibley, Lord John Manners and his Friends) (London, 1925), vol. I, p. 204n.

[62] This was a letter to his friend and fellow organizer of the Anti-Corn-Law League, George Wilson (John Morley, The Life of Richard Cobden (Boston, 1881), Feb. 28, 1852, p. 385.).

[63] Hansard, 3d ser., vol. 119, Feb. 27, 1852, 906.

[64] Ibid., vol. 121, Apr. 30, 1852, 12.

[65] Ibid., 55. Even The Times was impressed: "We saw with our own eyes the last rag of Protection put into a red box, and when the lid was opened, a perfect Chancellor of the Exchequer appeared..." (The Times, May 1, 1852).

[66] Hansard, 3d ser., vol. 121, Apr. 30, 1852, 58.

[67] Blake, Disraeli, p. 317.

[68]Hansard, 3d ser., vol. 121, May 7, 1852, 351-2.

[69]The judgement of The Times (April 5, 1852).

[70]Such an election ploy was provoking to The Times: it condemned the protectionists for appealing to the electorate "to support economical fallacies under the mask of religious verities" (The Times, July 19, 1852). The real issue, The Times declared, was "the question of Free Trade or Protection. All other considerations must be lost sight of, that this important point may be definitively set at rest" (The Times, July 5, 1852).

[71]Bucks Her., June 12, 1852.

[72]Blake, Disraeli, p. 319.

[73]Essex Std., July 16, 1852.

[74]Thomas Fricker (ed.) Poll Book of the North Lincolnshire Election taken in July 1852 (Boston, n.d.), p. xxv.

[75]Ibid., pp. xiv-xv.

[76]Lincolnshire Chr., Aug. 22, 1851.

[77]A discussion of the election and an analysis of the pollbook may be found in Olney, Lincolnshire Politics, pp. 121-39.

[78]Greville Memoirs, vol. 2, Aug. 2, 1852, p. 558.

[79]David Spring, "English Landed Society in the Eighteenth and Nineteenth Centuries," Econ. Hist. Rev., 2nd ser., vol. XVII, no. 1 (Aug. 1964), p. 152.

[80] Ronald Warren Linker, "Philip Pusey, Esquire: Country Gentleman, 1799-1855", Ph.D. Dissertation (Johns Hopkins, 1961), p. 578. The protectionist candidate was George Henry Vansittart of Bisham Abbey.

[81] John Allen, History of the Borough of Liskeard and its Vicinity (London, 1856), p. 475. I am grateful to the present owner of Pelyn, Nicholas Kendall, Esq., for the opportunity to examine the papers of his ancestor.

[82] Royal Cornwall Gazette, Dec. 13, 1850.

[83] Ibid., May 30, 1851.

[84] Ibid., Mar. 12, 1852.

[85] As in the election of 1847, uncertain party affiliations in the election of 1852 make it difficult to supply firm figures. Estimates of protectionist strength vary from a high of 347 to a low of 284. For a useful discussion of the election results, see J.B. Conacher, The Peelites and the Party System, 1846-52 (Newton Abbot,1972), pp 115 ff.

[86] This was Cobden's stated intention even before the session began. See Morley, Cobden's Life, letter to George Wilson, Aug. 18, 1852, p. 390.

[87] Hansard, 3d ser., vol. 123, Nov. 23, 1852, 351.

[88] Palmerston and some of the Peelites were willing to wait until Disraeli's budget proposals before making any irrevocable decisions about the continuance of the government (J.B. Conacher, The Aberdeen Coalition, 1852-1855 (Cambridge U. Press, 1968), p. 6).

[89]Hansard, 3d ser., vol. 123, Nov. 23, 1852, 451.

[90]Ibid., Nov. 25, 1852, 528-9.

[91]The Times, Dec. 2, 1852.

[92]For a discussion of the budget, see Blake, Disraeli, ch. XV; Halévy, Age of Peel and Cobden, pp. 285-87; F. Shehab, Progressive Taxation (Oxford, 1953), pp. 112-5. For the budget speech itself, see Hansard, 3d ser., vol. 123, Dec. 3, 1852, 836ff.

Chapter VII--Conclusion

Fortunately for Disraeli's position as leader (and for the
eventual re-constitution of the Conservative Party), protection was
not only dead in parliament, but was dying in the constituencies.
This was the direct consequence of three major economic developments.
First, beginning in mid-1852 agricultural prices rose significantly.
The next twenty years saw steady wheat prices and rising meat prices
as an accelerated population growth concentrated in the towns guaran-
teed an expanding urban market for agricultural products. Secondly,
the extension of the railways to all parts of the island provided op-
portunities for even the most remote farmer to reach these markets
easily and cheaply. Thirdly, by adopting increasingly sophisticated
agricultural improvements, farmers became more efficient. They learned
more about fertilizers and natural manures such as guano. They also
benefitted from the development of new mass production methods that,
for example, cheapened the cost of drainpipes. Many farmers adopted
the comprehensive system popularly known as high farming which was
based on heavy capital improvements (such as new farm buildings and
drainage) and on the extensive use of new feeds, fertilizers, and implements. Because high farming was based on lowering unit costs rather than being dependent upon high agricultural prices, and because
it was advocated by many free traders (including Peel), high farming
was at first viewed with some suspicion by protectionist farmers. But
when it was realized that increased production at lower costs could
sustain profits as well as less efficient methods in a protected

market, farmers came round. As farming improved so did profits--by
an estimated twenty-five percent on the whole from the early 1850's to
the late 1870's.[1]

As in the past, rural prosperity dampened discontent: farmers
lost interest in political agitation. In the affluent decades that
followed, farmers were once again willing to accept a traditional rural leadership. During the agitations between 1815 and 1852 farmers
had sought to convince the country leadership to protect agriculture
as it had always been protected. Only when their leaders seem to
desert them did farmers step out of their accustomed role. Therein
lay the weakness of the farmers as a pressure group. They wanted
things as they were. They had no vision of social or economic change.
They lacked a coherent and fully developed program. When profits returned, the uncongenial agitation faded naturally away.

Sporadic and inchoate as they may have been, the farmers' agitations had an undoubted impact upon local and national politics. They
influenced the outcome of elections and the decisions of members of
parliament. They provided the real strength of the protectionist
party, and thus brought down one of the most celebrated British minis-
tries. These farmers' agitations demonstrate clearly how political
influence in nineteenth century England sometimes worked from the
bottom upward.

Perhaps the most noteworthy long range effect of the farmers'
agitation was the very fact of their involvement in the politics of
an expanding political nation. In a country where public opinion was
becoming (in the words of The Times) "the one great agent of

Government and society," it was essential that both town and country
accept and practice the full apparatus of persuasion--petitions, meetings, newspapers, and organizations--to influence parliament. The
politics of public opinion could operate effectively only when interest
groups sought legitimate and widely recognized channels for the redress of their grievances. In this sense the fact that farmers failed
in their objectives is less important than the campaign they undertook.

Footnotes to Chapter VII

[1]Chambers and Mingay, <u>Agricultural Revolution</u>, p. 159. Other useful
references to the development of agriculture during its high Victorian period of prosperity are C. S. Orwin and E. H. Whetham, <u>History
of British Agriculture, 1846-1914</u> (1964); R. W. Sturgess, "The
Agricultural Revolution on the English Clays," <u>Agric. Hist. Rev.</u>,
Vol. XIV (1966), pt. II, 104-21; W. Harwood Long, "The Development of
Mechanization in English Farming," <u>Agric. Hist. Rev.</u>, vol. XI (1963),
pt. I; E. L. Jones, "The Changing Basis of English Agricultural
Prosperity, 1853-73," <u>Agric. Hist. Rev.</u>, vol X (1962), pt. II, 102-
19; G. E. Mingay," 'The Agricultural Revolution'" in English History:
A Reconsideration," <u>Agricultural History</u>, vol. 37, no. 3 (July, 1963),
pp. 123-33.

SELECT BIBLIOGRAPHY

This is not a comprehensive bibliography. It lists only those works referred to in the footnotes or in the appendices.

Manuscript Sources:
    Berkshire Record Office
      Benyon Papers
    British Museum
      Huskisson Papers, Add MSS 38, 742 and 38, 743
      Peel Papers, Add MSS 40443
      Young Papers, Add MSS 35, 133
    Cornwall Record Office
      Rashleigh MSS
      Rashleigh, Sir John Colman, bt., "Memoirs of Sir John Colman Rashleigh, Bt. in Four Parts (1772-1847)," in typescript
      Tithe Commutation Surveys 1842, 1843, 1844 of Cornwall
      Vyvyan Papers
    Essex Record Office
      Barret Lennard Correspondence
      Tabor, H.S., "History of the Tabor Family," (1917) in typescript ERO D/DTa Z6
    Hugenden, High Wycombe, Bucks
      Hughenden MSS
    Lincolnshire Record Office
      Ancaster MSS
      Monson MSS
    Pelyn, Cornwall
      Kendall MSS
    Public Record Office
      Ellenborough Papers, P.R.O. 30/12/1/6
      Home Office Papers, H.O./142

Parliamentary Publications
    Reports of Committee
      1816, VI, First Report of the Select Committee on Seeds and Wool.
      1820, II, Report from the Select Committee on Petitions Complaining of Agricultural Distress
      1821, IX, Report from the Select Committee to whom the several petitions complaining of the depressed state of the Agriculture of the United Kingdom, were referred.
      1822, V, Report from the Select Committee appointed to inquire into the Allegations of the several petitions presented to the house in the last and present sessions of Parliament, complaining of the distressed State of the Agriculture of the United Kingdom
      1836, VIII, First Report from the Select Committee appointed to inquire into the state of agriculture. Second Report from the Select Committee appointed to inquire into the state of agriculture.

1837-8, IX, Report on electors registered, and voters polled, at the last general election.

1846, VI, Select Committee of the House of Lords on the burdens affecting real property

1846, VIII, Report from the Select Committee on votes of electors.

1847-48, VII, Report from the Select Committee on agricultural customs.

1852-3, LXXXVIII, Census of Great Britain, 1851, Population Tables pts. 1 & 2.

Other Parliamentary Publications:

Hansard's Parliamentary Debates

Journals of the House of Commons and House of Lords

Statutes at Large

Poll Books, Voting Registers, Electoral Information:

Dod, Charles R., Electoral Facts from 1832 to 1852 (London, 1852).

Essex County Election (Chelmsford, n.d.), Essex R.O., D/DL 0 43/3

Essex, Northern Division, Copy of the Register of the Voters (Chelmsford, 1832)

Fricker, Thomas, Poll Book of the North Lincolnshire Election taken in July 1852 (Boston, n.d.).

Hinckford Agricultural and Conservative Club Broadsides, Essex R.O., D/DCM Z13.

"The Election in 1847 in South Essex," Essex R.O., D/DL 0 44/2

The Poll Book for the Election of Two Members to Represent in Parliament the Lindsey Division for Lincolnshire (Stamford, n.d.) (for 1835).

The Poll Book for the Parts of Lindsey in the County of Lincoln (1841).

Newspapers:

The Alfred

Berrow's Worcester Journal

Bristol Journal

Bristol Mercury

Bristol Observer

Bucks Herald

Bury Post

Cambridge Chronicle

Essex Standard

Farmers' Journal

Hampshire Telegraph

Hereford Journal

John Bull

Kentish Chronicle

Kentish Gazette

The League

Lincolnshire Chronicle

Morning Post
Norfolk Chronicle
Norfolk Yeoman's Gazette
Norwich Courier
Oxford Journal
Royal Cornwall Gazette
Salopian Journal
Stamford Mercury
Suffolk Chronicle
Taunton Courier
The Times
West Briton

Periodicals:
Annual Register
Cobbett's Weekley Political Register
Farmers' Magazine
Gentleman's Magazine
The Spectator
Pamphleteer

Pamphlets:
An Account of the Proceedings, Intentions, Resolutions, and
Premiums of the Essex Society for the Encouragement of Agri-
culture and Industry (Bocking, n.d.)
The Origin and Proceedings of the Agricultural Associations in
Great Britain (London, n.d.)
Western,C.C., Address to the Landowners of the United Empire
(London, 1822).

Autobiography, Biography and Correspondence:
Bacon, Richard Mackenzie, A Memoir of the Life of Edward, Third
Baron Suffield (Norwich, 1838).
Blake, Robert, Disraeli, (New York, 1967).
Brougham, Lord, The Life and Times of Henry Lord Brougham (New
York, 1871).
Buckingham and Chandos, Duke of, Memoirs of the Court of
George VI, 1820-30 (London, 1859).
Cobbett, William, Rural Rides, Everyman Edition (1912).
Cole, G.D.G., The Life of William Cobbett (London, 1925).
Creevy Papers, ed. Sir H. Maxwell, (New York, 1903).
The Croker Papers, ed. Louis J. Jennings (New York, 1884).
Disraeli, Benjamin, Lord George Bentinck: A Political Bio-
graphy (London, 1852).
The Greville Memoirs: A Journal of the Reigns of King George
IV and King William IV, ed. Henry Reeve (New York, 1875).
The Greville Memoirs (Second Part): A Journal of the Reign of
Queen Victoria, ed. Henry Reeve (New York, 1885).
Heron, Sir Robert, Notes (Grantham, 1850).
Hodder, Edwin, The Life and Work of the Seventh Earl of Shaftes-
bury, K.G. (London, 1886).

Knatchbull-Hugessen, Sir Hughe,Kentish Family (London, 1960)
Malmesbury, Earl of, Memoirs of an Ex-Minister: An Autobio-
    graphy (London, 1884), 2nd ed.
Mitchison, Rosalind, Agricultural Sir John (London, 1962)
Monypenny, William F. and Buckle, George, The Life of Benjamin
    Disraeli, Earl of Beaconsfield (New York, 1914). Vol. III
Morley, John, The Life of Richard Cobden (Boston, 1881).
Parker, Charles Stuart (ed.), Sir Robert Peel (London, 1899),
    Vol. II.
Parker, J. Oxley, The Oxley Parker Papers (Colchester, 1964).
Sraffa, P. (ed.), The Works and Correspondence of David Ricardo
    (Cambridge, 1952).
Stirling, A.M.W., Coke of Norfolk and His Friends (London,
    1912).
Twiss, H., The Public and Private Life of Lord Eldon (London,
    1844).
Wakefield, C.M., The Life of Thomas Attwood (London, 1885).
Wellington, Duke of (ed.), Despatches, Correspondence, and
    Memoranda of Field Marshall Arthur Duke of Wellington
    (London, 1867).
Whibley, Charles, Lord John Manners and his Friends (London,
    1925).

Secondary Works:
Acworth, A.W., Financial Reconstruction in England, 1815-1822
    (London, 1925).
Allen, John, History of the Borough of Liskeard and its
    Vicinity (London, 1856).
Anon., "The Provincial Press," Westminster Review, Vol. XII,
    (1830).
Barnes, Donald Grove, A History of the English Corn Laws from
    1660-1846 (New York, 1930).
Bischoff, James, A Comprehensive History of the Woollen and
    Worsted Manufacturers (London, 1842).
Blake, Robert, The Conservative Party from Peel to Churchill
    (New York, 1970).
Bourde, A.J., The Influence of England on the French Agronomes,
    1750-1789 (Cambridge, 1953).
Bovill, E.M., England in the Age of Nimrod and Surtees (Oxford
    UP, 1959).
Briggs, Asa, The Age of Improvement (London, 1959).
Chambers, J.D. and Mingay, G.E., The Agricultural Revolution,
    1750-1880 (London, 1966).
Christie, Ian R., "The Yorkshire Association, 1780-4: A Study
    in Political Organization," The Historical Journal, vol. III,
    no. 2 (1960).
Clarke, Sir Ernest, History of the Board of Agriculture, 1793-
    1833 (London, 1898).
Collins, E.J.T. and Jones, E.L., "Sectoral Advance in English
    Agriculture, 1850-1880", Agricultural Historical Review, XV,
    Pt. II (1967).

Conacher, J.B., _The Aberdeen Coalition 1852-1855_ (Cambridge, 1968).

Conacher, J.B., _The Peelites and the Party System, 1846-52_ (Newton Abbot, 1972).

Davies, E., "The Small Landowners, 1780-1832, in the Light of the Land Tax Assessments," _Econ. Hist. Rev._, 1st. ser., I (1927).

Davis, R.W., "Buckingham, 1832-1846: A Study of a Pocket Borough", _Huntington Library Quarterly_, Vol. XXXIV, No. 2 (February, 1971).

Davis, Richard W., _Political Change and Continuity, 1760-1885: A Buckinghamshire Study_ (Newton Abbot, 1972).

Dowell, Stephen, _A History of Taxation and Taxes in England_, 2nd (rev.), ed., (London, 1888).

Dunbabin, J.P.D., _Rural Discontent in Nineteenth-Century Britain_ (London, 1974).

Evans, George Ewart, _The Horse in the Furrow_ (London, 1960).

Feiling, K.G., _The Second Tory Party 1714-1832_ (London, 1951).

Fraser, Robert, _General View of the County of Cornwall_ (London, 1794).

Fussell, G.E., _More Old English Farming Books_ (London, 1950).

Fussell, G.E., and Compton, M., "Agricultural Adjustments after the Napoleonic Wars," _Econ. History_ III (1939).

Galpin, William F., _The Grain Supply of England During the Napoleonic Period_ (New York, 1925).

Gash, Norman, "Peel and the Party System," _Transactions of the Royal Historical Society_, 5th ser., vol. I (1951).

Gash, Norman, _Politics in the Age of Peel_ (London, 1953).

Gash, Norman, _Reaction and Reconstruction in English Politics, 1832-1852_ (Oxford, 1965).

Gayer, A.D., Rostow, W.W., and Schwartz, A.J., _The Growth and Fluctuation of the British Economy, 1780-1850_ (Oxford, 1953).

Gibbs, Sir B.T. Brandreth, _The Smithfield Club_, 3d ed. (London, 1881).

Grigg, David, _The Agricultural Revolution in South Lincolnshire_ (Cambridge, 1966).

Halevy, Elie, _A History of the English People in the Nineteenth Century_ 2d (rev.) ed., (New York, 1949) Vol. I, II, III.

Heaton, H., _The Yorkshire Woollen and Worsted Industries_ (Oxford, 1920).

Hennock, E.P., "The Sociological Premises of the First Reform Act: A Critical Note," _Victorian Studies_, Vol. XIV, no. 3 (March, 1971).

Hobsbawm, Eric and Rude, George, _Captain Swing_ (London, 1969)

Hughes, Edward, _Studies in Administration and Finance, 1558-1825_ (Manchester, 1934).

Imlah, A.H., _Economic Elements in the Pax Britannica_ (Harvard, 1958).

John, A.H., "The Course of Agricultural Change, 1660-1760," in L.S. Pressnell (ed.), _Studies in the Industrial Revolution_ (London, 1960).

John, A.H.,"Farming in Wartime: 1793-1815," in E.L. Jones and
G.E. Mingay (eds.), Land, Labour, and Population in the
Industrial Revolution (London, 1967).

Jones, E.L., "The Changing Basis of English Agricultural Prosperity, 1853-73," Agricultural History Review, Vol. X (1962),
pt. II.

Jones, E.L., Seasons and Prices: the Role of the Weather in
English Agricultural History (London, 1964).

Jones, Wilbur Devereux and Erickson, Arvel B., The Peelites,
1846-1857 (Ohio State, 1972).

Karkeek, W.F., "On the Farming of Cornwall," Journal of the
Royal Agricultural Society of England (1845), pt. 2.

Keith-Lucas, B., "County Meetings," Law Quarterly Rev., Vol.
LXX (Jan., 1954).

Kemp, Betty, "The General Election of 1841," History, vol.
XXXVIII, no. 130 (June, 1952).

Kerridge, Eric, The Agricultural Revolution (London, 1967).

Lance, E.J., The Hop Farmer (London, 1838).

Lawson-Tancred, Mary, "The Anti-League and the Corn Law Crisis
of 1846," Historical Journal, vol. III, no. 2 (1960).

Lewis, William, A Century of Agricultural Progress (Bath, 1879).

Lipson, E., A Short History of Wool and its Manufacture
(London, 1953).

Long, W. Harwood, "The Development of Mechanization in English
Farming," Agricultural History Review, vol. XI (1963), pt. 1.

McCord, Norman, The Anti-Corn Law League (London, 1968) 2d ed.

Marshall, William, The Rural Economy of Norfolk (London, 1787),
Vol. I.

Marshall, William, The Rural Economy of the Midland Counties
(London, 1790).

Marshall, William, The Rural Economy of the West of England
(London, 1796), Vol. I.

Mathias, Peter, The Brewing Industry in England, 1700-1830
(Cambridge, 1959).

Mingay, G.E., English Landed Society in the Eighteenth Century
(London, 1963).

Mingay, G.E., "'The Agricultural Revolution' in English History,"
Agricultural History, Vol. 37, No. 3 (July, 1963).

Mingay, G.E., Enclosure and the Small Farmer in the Age of the
Industrial Revolution (London, 1968).

Mitchison, Rosalind, "The Old Board of Agriculture (1793-1822),"
English Historical Review, Vol. LXXIV (1959).

Moore, D.C., "The Corn Laws and High Farming," Economic History
Review, 2nd ser., Vol. XVIII, No. 3 (Dec., 1965).

Moore, D.C., "Social Structure, Political Structure, and Public
Opinion in Mid-Victorian England," in Robert Robson (ed.),
Ideas and Institutions of Victorian England (New York, 1967).

Mosse, George L., "The Anti-League: 1844-1846," Economic History
Review, Vol. XVII, No. 2 (1947).

Olney, R.J., Lincolnshire Politics, 1832-1885 (Oxford, 1973).

Orwin, C.S. and Whetham, E.H., History of British Agriculture,
1846-1914 (1964).

Osborne, John W., "William Cobbett and the Corn Laws," The Historian, Vol. XXIX, no. 2 (Feb. 1967).

Parker, Hubert H., The Hop Industry (London, 1934).

Peacock, A.J., Bread or Blood (London, 1965).

Perkins, J.A., "Tenure, Tenant Right, and Agricultural Progress in Lindsey, 1780-1850," Agricultural History Review, Vol. XXIII, pt. 1 (1975).

Pressnell, L.S., Country Banking in the Industrial Revolution (Oxford, 1956).

Prince, H.C., "The Tithe Surveys of the Mid-Nineteenth Century," Agricultural History Review, Vol. VII (1959), pt. I.

Riches, N., The Agricultural Revolution in Norfolk (Chapel Hill, 1937).

Robson, R., The Attorney in Eighteenth Century England (Cambridge, 1959).

Rowe, John, Cornwall in the Age of the Industrial Revolution (Liverpool, 1953).

Schuyler, R.L., The Fall of the Old Colonial System: A Study in British Free Trade, 1770-1870 (New York, 1945).

Schuyler, R.L., "British Imperial Preference and Sir Robert Peel," Political Science Quarterly, Vol. XXXII, no. 3 (Sept. 1917).

Shehab, F., Progressive Taxation (Oxford, 1953).

Smart, William, Economic Annals of the Nineteenth Century (London, 1910-17).

Spring, David, The English Landed Estate in the Nineteenth Century: Its Administration (Baltimore, 1963).

Spring, David, "English Landed Society in the Eighteenth and Nineteenth Centuries," Economic History Review, 2d ser., Vol. XVII, no. 1 (August, 1964).

Spring, David, "Lord Chandos and the Farmers, 1818-1846," Huntington Library Quarterly, Vol. XXXIII, no. 3 (May, 1970).

Spring, David and Eileen, "The Fall of the Grenville, 1844-1848," Huntington Library Quarterly, Vol. XIX, no. 2 (February, 1956).

Spring, David and Crosby, Travis L., "George Webb Hall and the Agricultural Association," Jnl. of British Studies, Vol. 1, No. 1 (Nov, 1962).

Stewart, Robert, The Politics of Protection (Cambridge, 1971)

Sturgess, R.W., "The Agricultural Revolution on the English Clays," Agricultural History Review, Vol. XIV (1966), pt. II.

Thirsk, Joan, English Peasant Farming: The Agrarian History of Lincolnshire from Tudor to Present Times (London, 1957).

Thompson, F.M.L., "The End of a Great Estate," Economic History Review, 2nd Ser., Vol. VIII, No. 1 (August, 1955)

Thompson, F.M.L., "Whigs and Liberals in the West Riding," English Historical Review, Vol. LXXIV (1959).

Thompson, F.M.L., "Landownership and Economic Growth in England in the Eighteenth Century," in E.L. Jones and S.J. Woolf (eds.), Agrarian Change and Economic Development (London, 1960).

Thompson, F.M.L., English Landed Society in the Nineteenth Century (London, 1963).

Thompson, F.M.L., "The Social Distribution of Landed Property in England since the Sixteenth Century," _Economic History Review_, 2nd Ser., Vol. XIX, No, 3 (1966).

Thompson, F.M.L., "The Second Agricultural Revolution, 1815-1880," _Economic History Review_, 2nd Ser., Vol. XXI, No. 1 (April, 1968).

Trow-Smith, Robert, _A History of the British Livestock Industry, 1700-1900_ (London, 1959).

Venn, J.A. _Foundations of Agricultural Economics_ (Cambridge, 1923).

Ward, W.R., "The Tithe Question in England in the Early Nineteenth Century," _Journal of Ecclesiastical History_, Vol. XVI, No. 1 (Apr. 1965).

Worgan, G.B., _General View of the Agriculture of the County of Cornwall_ (London, 1811).

Unpublished theses and dissertations:

Chesher, V.M., "Some Cornish Landowners, 1690-1760: A Social and Economic Study" (Oxford Thesis, 1957).

Cox, Elwyn A., "An Agricultural Geography of Essex, c. 1840," (University of London M.A. Thesis, 1963).

Cunningham, Susan E., "Changes in the Pattern of Rural Settlement in Northern Essex between 1650 and 1850," (Victoria University of Manchester, M.A. Thesis, 1968).

Elvins, W. Brian, "The Reform Movement and County Politics in Cornwall, 1809-1852" (University of Birmingham M.A. Thesis, 1959).

Linker, R.W., "Philip Pusey Esquire: Country Gentlemen, 1799-1855" (Johns Hopkins Ph.D. dissertation, 1961).

Obelkevitch, James, "Religion and Rural Society in South Lindsey, 1825-75," (Columbia University Ph.D. Dissertation, 1971).

Pollock, Norman H., "The English Game Laws in the Nineteenth Century" (Johns Hopkins University Ph.D. dissertation, 1968).

Shrimpton, Colin, "The Landed Society and the Farming Community of Essex in the late Eighteenth and Early Nineteenth Centuries," (Trinity Hall, Cambridge, Ph.D. dissertation, 1965).

Veliz, Claudio, "Arthur Young and the English Landed Interest, 1784-1813" (London School of Economics, Ph.D. Thesis, 1959).

APPENDIX I

The information below is taken from Report on Electors Registered, and Voters
Polled, at the last General Election, <u>Parlimentary Papers</u> (1838), IX. Bedford,
Berkshire, and Somerset were omitted because their returns were not itemized
into the separate categories of freeholder, leaseholder, copyholder, and occupier.
In some counties the total column does not match the total number of electors in
the four categories. This is usually due to an intentional omission of a fifth
column in the original report, headed "other," that did not seem relevant to
our purposes here.

County	freeholder	categories leaseholder	copyholder	occupier	total
Bedford	-	-	-	-	-
Berkshire	-	-	-	-	-
Buckinghamshire	4198	53	277	1154	5689
Cambridge	2813	25	573	564	4013
Chester, North	2948	887	200	1605	6029
Chester, South	4038	390	12	2278	7084
Cornwall, East	2710	1237	196	1218	5469
Cornwall, West	1814	2195	46	828	4928
Cumberland, East[a]	2559	1447	96	-	4638
Cumberland, West[a]	3007	1073	64	-	4437
Devon, North	4482	1117	93	2065	7757
Devon, South	6187	1660	159	2769	10775
Derby, North	3858	261	167	1226	5527
Derby, South	4462	37	280	1539	6575
Dorset	3853	491	436	1396	6263
Durham	6431	432	806	2143	10305
Essex, North	3672	90	881	1256	5899
Essex, South	3000	211	831	1505	5547
Gloucester, East	6125	178	196	1184	7683
Gloucester, West	5362	230	96	1316	7004
Hampshire	6597	374	905	1331	9214
Hereford	5324	76	199	1572	7216
Hertford	3218	51	781	1195	5245
Huntingdon	1747	6	368	566	2805
Kent, East	5999	207	14	1073	7293
Kent, West	6426	411	25	1570	8432

a. There was no separate occupier category listed; these were included in the leasehold category.

County electors in 1837

County	categories				
	freeholder	leaseholder	copyholder	occupier	total
Lancaster, North	5088	403	903	3256	9691
Lancaster, South	11581	2424	362	3140	17754
Leicester, North	3160	15	19	1053	4299
Leicester, South	3450	5	130	965	4580
Lincoln, Holland	2803	6	218	983	4010
Lincoln, Kesteven	2323	-	307	1392	4090
Lincoln, Lindsey	6564	35	441	3053	10141
Middlesex	9485	1068	975	1292	12820
Monmouth	2466	418	339	991	4347
Norfolk, East	5225	31	892	1773	8343
Norfolk, West	4271	8	932	1701	7258
Northampton, North	2263	15	508	998	3857
Northampton, South	3357	26	146	1023	4600
Northumberland, North	1520	-	56	1050	2786
Northumberland, South	3377	-	202	2145	5070
Nottingham, North	2618	29	390	448	3608
Nottingham, South	2291	35	239	955	3621
Oxford	3705	131	300	1114	5253
Rutland[b]	1022	8	-	307	1337
Salop, North & South	5367	121	203	2637	8414
Somerset	-	-	-	-	-
Stafford, North	6934	128	368	2107	9540
Stafford, South	5758	182	473	1434	7871
Suffolk, East	3780	34	750	1624	6278
Suffolk, West	3139	15	539	1196	4959

b. Copyholders were included in the freeholder category.

| County | categories | | | | |
	freeholder	leaseholder	copyholder	occupier	total
Surrey, East	3679	664	287	901	5531
Surrey, West	2516	85	501	586	3688
Sussex, East	3060	56	652	892	4799
Sussex, West	2068	131	335	427	3152
Warwick, North	5031	407	143	1050	6632
Warwick, South	2869	82	62	1291	4304
Westmorland[c]	-	-	-	-	4683
Wilts, North	3755	163	255	895	5068
Wilts, South	1878	317	127	640	2962
Worcester, East	4592	132	240	970	5995
Worcester, West	3326	215	186	856	4654
Yorkshire, East Riding	4152	34	573	2421	7180
Yorkshire, North Riding	7448	208	489	4399	11716
Yorkshire, West Riding	19670	1011	1349	6023	29076

c. Westmorland's categories were divided thus: landed property -- 3662; farmers -- 934.

APPENDIX II

The information for the following chart is taken from <u>Essex, Northern</u> <u>Division, Copy of the Register of the Voters,</u> (Chelmsford, 1832). Penned in ink are the results of the poll, presumably made by an election officer. This may account for the fact that the totals given here do not agree with the official number at the close of the poll. According to this source Western received more votes than Baring, which would have put him in the winner's column. In fact Baring and Tyrell were the victors. This discrepancy does not detract from our purpose in illustrating the importance of the fifty pound occupiers to the Conservative victors. If the fifty pound occupier category is omitted, the election results would have been: Tyrell -- 1872, Western -- 1795, Baring -- 1670, Brand -- 1489.

Essex, Northern Division, 1832.   Total number of votes cast.

	number voters	number votes	number of votes cast for				number of plumpers for			
			Tyrell	Baring	Western	Brand	T	B	W	Br
ESSEX (total)										
all	4455	8712	2440	2206	2237	1829	82	32	71	12
₤50	970	1886	568	536	442	340	21	9	21	3
CLAVERING										
all	86	167	41	35	48	43	4	0	1	0
₤50	14	25	8	5	7	5	2	0	0	0
DUNMOW										
all	390	764	211	195	186	172	9	2	2	2
₤50	126	227	70	65	46	46	5	0	0	1
FRESHWELL										
all	169	332	98	88	77	69	4	0	1	1
₤50	50	101	30	26	24	21	3	0	0	0
HINCKFORD										
all	1066	2095	599	552	498	446	17	3	12	5
₤50	182	356	108	99	81	68	1	0	5	2
LEXDEN										
all	913	1780	478	399	499	404	14	11	19	2
₤50	137	269	83	75	63	48	1	2	2	0
TENDRING										
all	699	1354	416	428	308	202	8	14	22	0
₤50	205	390	120	131	91	48	3	7	10	0
THURSTABLE										
all	203	400	103	76	137	84	1	0	3	1
₤50	48	96	24	26	28	18	0	0	0	0
UTTLESFORD										
all	496	969	234	216	268	251	15	1	6	1
₤50	98	190	50	44	51	45	3	0	3	0
WINSTREE										
all	106	207	81	70	34	22	3	0	2	0
₤50	33	65	22	19	13	11	1	0	0	0
WITHAM										
all	328	644	179	147	182	136	7	1	4	0
₤50	85	167	53	46	38	30	2	0	1	0

Essex, Northern Division, 1832.   Percentages of votes cast.

	total no. votes	percentage of votes cast going to				percentage of voters plumping for			
		T	B	W	Br	T	B	W	Br
ESSEX (total)									
all voters	8712	28.01	25.32	25.68	20.99	1.84	0.72	1.59	0.27
₤50	1886	30.12	28.42	23.44	18.03	2.16	0.93	2.16	0.31
CLAVERING									
all voters	167	24.55	20.96	28.74	25.75	4.65	0.00	1.17	0.00
₤50	25	32.00	20.00	28.00	20.00	14.29	0.00	0.00	0.00
DUNMOW									
all voters	764	27.62	25.52	24.35	22.51	2.31	0.51	0.51	0.51
₤50	227	30.84	28.63	20.26	20.26	3.97	0.00	0.00	0.79
FRESHWELL									
all voters	332	29.52	26.51	23.19	20.78	2.37	0.00	0.59	0.59
₤50	101	29.70	25.74	23.76	20.79	5.77	0.00	0.00	0.00
HINCKFORD									
all voters	2095	28.59	26.35	23.77	21.29	1.59	0.28	1.13	0.47
₤50	356	30.34	27.81	22.75	19.10	0.55	0.00	2.75	1.10
LEXDEN									
all voters	1780	26.85	22.42	28.03	22.70	1.53	1.20	2.08	0.22
₤50	269	30.86	27.88	23.42	17.84	0.73	1.46	1.46	0.00
TENDRING									
all voters	1354	30.72	31.61	22.75	14.92	1.14	2.00	3.15	0.00
₤50	390	30.77	33.59	23.33	12.31	1.46	3.41	4.88	0.00
THURSTABLE									
all voters	400	25.75	19.00	34.25	21.00	0.49	0.00	1.48	0.49
₤50	96	25.00	27.08	29.17	18.75	0.00	0.00	0.00	0.00
UTTLESFORD									
all voters	969	24.15	22.29	27.66	25.90	3.02	0.20	1.21	0.20
₤50	190	26.32	23.16	26.84	23.68	3.06	0.00	3.06	0.00
WINSTREE									
all voters	207	39.13	33.82	16.43	10.63	2.83	0.00	1.87	0.00
₤50	65	33.85	29.23	20.00	16.92	3.03	0.00	0.00	0.00
WITHAM									
all voters	644	27.80	22.83	28.26	21.12	2.13	0.30	1.22	0.00
₤50	167	31.74	27.54	22.75	17.96	2.35	0.00	1.18	0.00

APPENDIX III

In the Cabinet

First Lord of the Treasury	Earl of Derby
Lord Chancellor	Lord St. Leonards
Chancellor of the Exchequer	Benjamin Disraeli
President of the Council	Earl of Lonsdale
Privy Seal	Marquess of Salisbury
Home Secretary	Spencer Horatio Walpole
Foreign Secretary	Earl of Malmesbury
Colonial Secretary	Sir John Somerset Pakington, Bart.
First Lord of the Admiralty	Duke of Northumberland
President of the Board of Control	John Charles Herries
Postmaster General	Earl of Hardwicke
President of the Board of Trade	Joseph Warner Henley
First Commissioner of Works and Public Buildings	Lord John James Robert Manners

Not in the Cabinet

Commander in Chief	Duke of Wellington
Master General of the Ordnance	Viscount Hardinge
Paymaster of the Forces, and Vice-President of the Board of Trade	Lord Colchester
Secretary at War	William Beresford
Chancellor of the Duchy of Lancester	Robert Adam Christopher
Joint Secretaries of the Treasury	William Forbes Mackenzie, Esq., and George Alexander Hamilton, Esq.
Secretary of the Admiralty	Stafford Augustus O'Brien Stafford, Esq.
Under Secretary for the Home Department	Sir William Hylton Jolliffe, Bart.
Under Secretary for Foreign Affairs	Lord Stanley
Under Secretary for the Colonies	Earl of Desart
Secretaries of the Board of Control	Charles Lennox Cumming Bruce, Esq., and Henry James Baillie, Esq.

Lords of the Treasury	Marquess of Chandos, Lord Henry George Charles Gordon Lennc and Thomas Bateson, Esq.
Lords of the Admiralty	Rear Admiral Hyde Parker, C.B., Rear Admiral Phipps Hornby, C.B., Captain Sir Thomas Herbert, K.C.B., Captain Hon. Arthur Duncombe, and Captain Alexander Milne
Clerk of Ordnance	Colonel Francis Plunket Dunne
Attorney General	Sir Frederick Thesiger, Knt.
Solicitor General	Sir FitzRoy Kelly, Knt.
Judge-Advocate General	George Bankes
Chief Poor Law Commissioner	Sir John Trollope, Bart.

APPENDIX IV

To give point to our contention that farmers and gentry were very active in county meetings during the years 1830 - 1852, the following lists have been drawn up for one county. List A includes those agricultural societies which met in Cornwall during the years 1830 - 1852 as reported in the Royal Cornwall Gazette and the West Briton. Very probably not all meetings appeared in print; this list must therefore be considered the minimum number that actually met. The meetings were sometimes termed associations, sometimes societies; the names are listed here as given. List B includes some farmers and gentry active in these societies.

Cornwall has been chosen as a representative sample for two independent reasons. First, as one of the least noted agricultural counties, there were likely fewer agricultural meetings in Cornwall than in most other counties hence giving a desirable conservative bias to our sample. Second, the principal method used to identify the farmers and gentry is the tithe commutation survey of the 1840's (located at the Cornwall Record Office in Truro). Since the survey covers 98.6% of Cornwall's area -- a higher percentage than in most counties -- the likelihood of identifying the farmers and gentry in Cornwall was greater than for other counties (see H.C. Prince, "The Tithe Surveys of the Mid-Nineteenth Century," Agric. Hist. Rev., vol VII (1959), pt. I, pp. 14 - 26.)

List A: Agricultural Meetings in Cornwall, 1830 - 1852.   213

year	meetings

1830   Cornwall Agricultural Association
        Penwith Agricultural Society

1831   Cornwall Agricultural Association
        Penwith Agricultural Society

1832   Cornwall Agricultural Association
        Kirrier Agricultural Society

1833   Cornwall Agricultural Association
        East Cornwall Agricultural Society
        Penwith Agricultural Association (met twice this year)

1834   Cornwall Agricultural Association
        Roseland Agricultural Association

1835   Roseland Agricultural Association

1836   Cornwall Agricultural Association (met twice this year)
        East Cornwall and Roborough Agricultural Association
        Kirrier Agricultural Society
        Meneage Agricultural Society
        Penwith Agricultural Association
        Roseland Agricultural Association
        Veryan Plowing Match

1837   East Cornwall and Roborough Agricultural Society

1838   Cornwall Agricultural Association
        East Cornwall and Roborough Agricultural Society
        Roseland Agricultural Association

1839   Cornwall Agricultural Association (met twice this year)
        Hayle Agricultural Association
        Probus Agricultural Association (this association apparently met
              every month)
        Roseland Agricultural Association

1840   Cornwall Agricultural Association
        East Cornwall Agricultural Association
        Illogan Farmers' Club (met twice this year)
        Kirrier Agricultural Society
        Launceston Farmers' Association
        Penwith Agricultural Association
        Probus Agricultural Association
        Roseland Agricultural Association
        Stratton Agricultural Association
        Stythians Agricultural Society
        Veryan Farmers' Club

<u>year</u>   <u>meetings</u>

1841   Cornwall Agricultural Association (met three times this year)
          East Cornwall and Roborough Agricultural Society (met twice this year)
          East Penwith Agricultural Society
          Illogan Farmers' Club
          Kirrier Agricultural Society
          Penwith Agricultural Society
          Pydar Farmers' Club
          Roseland Agricultural Association
          St. Columb Farmers' Club
          Stratton Agricultural Society
          Wadebridge Farmers' Club
          West Devon and East Cornwall Agricultural Association

1842   East Penwith Agricultural Society
          Kirrier Agricultural Society
          Lostwithiel Agricultural Society
          Penwith Agricultural Society
          Probus Farmers' Club
          Stratton Agricultural Society

1843   Cardynham Agricultural Association
          East Cornwall and Roborough Agricultural Society
          East Penwith Agricultural Association
          Kirrier Agricultural Association
          Lostwithiel Agricultural Meeting
          Penwith Agricultural Association
          Probus Farmers' Club
          St. Austell Farmers' Club
          St. Columb Farmers' Club
          St. Germans Farming Club
          Stratton Agricultural Society
          Wadebridge Farmers' Club

1844   Cornwall Agricultural Association (met twice this year)
          East Cornwall Agricultural Society
          East Cornwall Experimental Club (met three times this year)
          East Penwith Agricultural Society
          Kirrier Agricultural Society
          Launceston Agricultural Society
          Lifton Park Sheep Shearing and Cattle Show
          Lostwithiel Agricultural Society
          North Cornwall Experimental Club (met four times this year)
          Penwith Agricultural Society
          Probus Farmers' Club
          Roseland Agricultural Association
          Stratton Agricultural Society
          Trigg Agricultural Society

1845   Cornwall Agricultural Society
          Trigg Agricultural Society

1846   St. Austell Farmers' Club

<u>year</u>   <u>meetings</u>

1847   East Cornwall Agricultural Society
            Probus Farmers' Club
            Trigg Agricultural Society

1848   Callington Agricultural Meeting
            Kirrier Agricultural Society
            St. Germans Farmers' Club
            Stratton Agricultural Society
            Stythians Agricultural Society

1849   Boscastle and Camelford Agricultural Society
            Callington Agricultural Association
            Cornwall Agricultural Association
            St. Tudy Plowing Match

1850   Cornwall Agricultural Association (met twice this year)
            East Cornwall Agricultural Society
            Kirrier Agricultural Society
            Penwith Agricultural Society
            Probus Plowing Match
            St. Germans Agricultural Society (met twice this year)
            Trigg Agricultural Society
            Wadebridge Farmers' Club (met twice this year)

1851   Callington Agricultural Association
            Cornwall Agricultural Association (met twice this year)
            East Cornwall Agricultural Association
            Kirrier Agricultural Society
            Penwith Agricultural Society
            Probus Farmers' Club
            St. Germans Farmers' Club
            Trigg Agricultural Society

1852   Cornwall Agricultural Association
            Probus Plowing Match
            Trigg Agricultural Society
            Wadebridge Farmers' Club

List B: Some farmers and gentry active in Cornish agricultural meetings

G. Andrew of Carne, vice-president of the St. Austell Farmers' Club in
1843, was a tenant of 110 acres.

H.P. Andrew of Bodrean, president of the Cornwall Agricultural Association
in 1844 and 1850, owned 413 acres of which he farmed eighty-nine; the remainder
was leased out.

D.D. Badcock of Swannacott, Week St. Mary, at one time vice-president
of the Stratton Agricultural Society, leased one farm of 388 acres from
Lady Bassett and another twenty-two acres from other landlords.

Thomas Baker of Cartuther, who once spoke at an agricultural meeting
at Liskeard in 1849, occupied 357 acres.

Deeble Boger, president of the Callington Agricultural Association in
1851, farmed sixty-seven acres, leasing another forty-seven acres to another
farmer.

Francis Cross, chairman of a St. Eval (near St. Columb) meeting in January,
1841, favoring the Corn Laws, owned more than 445 acres.

John Dingle of Darley spoke at the Trigg Agricultural Society in 1850;
he farmed 221 acres of his own and leased another eleven acres from the Duchy
of Cornwall.

J.S. Enys of Enys presided at the 1841 meeting of the Cornwall Agricultural
Association; he owned 350 acres in the parish of St. Gluvias.

William Foster of Lanwithan, who spoke at the Lostwithiel Agricultural
Society in 1842, owned sixty-one acres and rented another thirteen in the
parish of St. Winnow.

John Gilbert of Trelissick (Feock), chaired the Cornwall Agricultural
Association in 1849; he purchased his land--about 1000 acres--from Lord
Falmouth a few years previously (R. Symon, A Geographical Dictionary
or Gazeteer of the County of Cornwall (Penzance, 1884), p. 117).

James Glanville, who spoke at the county meeting of 1850, farmed 400
acres in St. Enoder (Royal Corn. Gaz., Feb. 15, 1850).

J. Hendy presided over a meeting of the Cornwall Agricultural Association
in 1851; he owned 511 acres in the parish of Ladock.

F. J. Hext, chairman of the Trigg Agricultural Society in 1852, owned
209 acres and leased another thirty-two in the parish of St. Mabyn.

T. Liddell spoke for small farmers at the Wadebridge Farmers' Club in
1850; he leased 125 acres in Minver parish.

Olver of Trescow, who spoke at the county meeting of 1850, was a tenant of 500 acres in St. Mabyn (Royal Corn. Gaz., Feb. 15, 1850).

William Palmer, a vice-chairman of the St. Germans Farmers' Club, rented 228 acres from the Earl of St. Germans.

J. Coryton Roberts of Trevol was vice-chairman of the Callington Agricultural Association in 1849; he leased 591 acres and owned fifty-nine more.

W.B. Snell of Landulph, who presided at the Callington Agricultural meeting in 1848, occupied 184 acres and owned 106 more.

George Stephens of Hengar, who spoke at the Trigg Agricultural meeting in 1845, leased 128 acres and owned another nine.

W. Symons of Hatt, who was president of the St. Germans Farmers' Club in 1851, owned 213 acres in Botusfleming parish, of which he farmed forty-one himself, leasing out the remainder.

Robert Taylor of St. Cleer, who was active in the East Cornwall Society for the Protection of Native Industry, owned 150 acres.

William Vosper, a vice-chairman of the St. Germans Farmers' Club, rented 287 acres from the Earl of St. Germans.

APPENDIX V

Wheat Prices from 1800 to 1855

The prices from 1800 to 1850 were taken from D.G. Barnes, A History of the English Corn Laws (New York, 1930), p. 298. The prices from 1851 to 1855 were calculated from information in the Annual Register for those years.

year	price per quarter		year	price per quarter		year	price per quarter	
	s.	d.		s.	d.		s.	d.
1800	113	10	1823	53	4	1846	54	8
1801	119	6	1824	63	11	1847	69	9
1802	69	10	1825	68	6	1848	50	6
1803	58	10	1826	58	8	1849	44	3
1804	62	3	1827	58	6	1850	40	3
1805	89	9	1828	60	5	1851	38	8
1806	79	1	1829	66	3	1852	40	7
1807	75	4	1830	64	3	1853	53	4
1808	81	4	1831	66	4	1854	68	9
1809	97	4	1832	58	8	1855	74	9
1810	106	5	1833	52	11			
1811	95	3	1834	46	2			
1812	126	6	1835	39	4			
1813	109	9	1836	48	6			
1814	74	4	1837	55	10			
1815	65	7	1838	64	7			
1816	78	6	1839	70	8			
1817	96	11	1840	66	4			
1818	86	3	1841	64	4			
1819	74	6	1842	57	3			
1820	67	10	1843	50	1			
1821	56	1	1844	51	3			
1822	44	7	1845	50	10			

INDEX

Agricultural depression, 9,
    26, 28, 34, 85-6, 156
Agricultural protection, 17,
    Ch. II, _passim_
Agricultural societies, 11, 12
Albemarle, 4th earl of, 62-3
Anti-Corn Law League, 130
Anti-League, 130, 136-38
Ashley, Lord, 138
Attwood, Thomas, 44-5

Baker, T., 127
Baker, Robert, 131, 138
Ball, Edward, 169, 174
Bankes, George, 140
Baring, Alexander, 98, 99
Barrow, William, 164-5
Bawtree, John, 122
Bedford, 6th duke of, 64
Bentinck, Lord George, 141,
    154-5
Beresford, William, 155,
    168-9
Biddle, Arthur, 6
Blackstone, W. S., 128
Bligh, John Martin, 39
Boger, Deeble, 124

Bourn Agricultural Society, 128
Bramston, T. W., 123
Brickwell, John, 39
Buckingham Agricultural Pro-
    tection Society, 137
Buckinghamshire: election of
    1832 in, 92
Buckinghamshire Agricultural
    Association, 89
Bucks Herald, 93, 119, 169

Cambridgeshire Farmers'
    Association, 174
Cambridgeshire Protection
    Society, 137
Canadian Corn Bill (1843), 126
Canning, George, 81
Cayley, E. S., 157, 177
Central Association, 35-40, 44-5
Chandos, Marquis of, 84, 88-90
    93-4, 96
Chandos Clause, 84-5
Chelmsford Farmers' Club,
    127
Christopher, R. A., 117, 138
Cobbett, William, 46, 57-8,
    67-73

Fane, John, 40

Farmers: economic power of, 2-3;
  as tenants, 4; status of, 6;
  and landlords, 8, 9; and provincial newspapers, 12; and
  taxes, 13-4; and tithes, 14-5;
  and currency question, 16;
  and parliamentary reform, 16;
  and agricultural protection,
  17, 18; and corn law of 1815,
  27-8; and reform campaign of
  1822, 65-6; radical spirit
  of, 71-3; suspicion of,
  toward whigs, 82-3; and
  Bucks election of 1835, 92-5;
  opposition of, to corn law
  revision (1842), 122-5; opposition of, toward Canadian
  Corn Bill (1843), 127; and
  protectionist agitation
  (1849-50), 162-3; and election
  of 1851, 173-4; prosperity
  of, 187-8

Farmers' Journal, 26, 28, 34,
  36-7, 43

Femantle, Sir Thomas, 138

Gem, Harvey, 9

Gloucester and Somerset
  Association, 33

Gooch, T. S., 42

Granby, marquis of, 155

Grey, 2nd earl, 61

Grosvenor, R. D., 40

Hamilton, Capt. Charles J.B.,
  124

Handley, Henry, 116

Harvey, R. C., 38, 45

Heron, Sir Robert, 65

Hildyard, Thomas, 137

Hinckford Agricultural and Conservative
  Club, 99, 126, 130-1

Holme Sumner, George, 40

Hop tax, 14

Horncastle Agricultural Protection Society, 138

Huskisson, William, 41, 65-6

Iles, F., 122

Jacob, William, 42

Jersey, 5th earl of, 63

Jonas, Samuel, 8

Kendall, Nicholas, 174-5